A STRUGGLE FOR FAME
Victorian Women Artists and Authors

Susan P. Casteras and Linda H. Peterson

Yale Center for British Art
New Haven, Connecticut
1994

Published on the occasion of an exhibition
at the Yale Center for British Art
March 1 – May 8, 1994

© 1994 by the Yale Center for British Art
Library of Congress Catalogue Card No. 94-060143
ISBN 0-930606-72-8

Designed and typeset by Julie Lavorgna
Photography by Richard Caspole
Prepared for press by GIST, Inc.
Printed by Van Dyck Columbia

Cover:
Florence Claxton (fl. 1855–1879)
Conversazione
Illustration for "A Conversazione at Willis's
Rooms: 'The Artists' and Amateurs' Society'"
for *London Society,* 1862
Engraving

TABLE OF CONTENTS

ACKNOWLEDGMENTS
ೇೊ-ೇೊ-ೇೊ-ೇೊ-ೇೊ-ೇೊ-ೇೊ-ೇೊ-ೇೊ-ೇೊ-ೇೊ-ೇೊ-ೇೊ-ೇೊ-ೇೊ

A Struggle for Fame is the result of felicitous cooperation on many levels between the co-authors and co-organizers with numerous others at Yale University and beyond. Since the exhibition is drawn mainly from the riches of Yale's holdings, we are particularly indebted to colleagues at the Center and elsewhere in the University who helped us to realize this project. At the Center there are many people to be warmly thanked: above all, Julie Lavorgna, who masterfully transformed our text into a proper catalogue; Tim Goodhue, who expedited all loan arrangements; the technical staff of Rick Johnson, Chick Cerillo, Don Rogers, and others who facilitated the installation of the show; and Marilyn Hunt and Richard Caspole for their expert handling of photography. We are grateful for the excellent support received from Patrick Noon, Scott Wilcox, and Elisabeth Fairman, and our colleagues Theresa Fairbanks, Julie Dennin, and Kimberly Rannala. We very much appreciate the many tasks performed by Kimberly Kneeland in the Paintings Department. Former colleagues Charlotte Saenz-Boldt and Caroline Prymas contributed to early research efforts, and Audrey Healy in the English Department also helped in keeping this project on schedule.

Also at the University, the Beinecke Rare Book and Manuscript Library has once again been enormously generous with its loans, and we sincerely thank Ralph W. Franklin and Vincent Giroud, as well as Millicent Abell, Gisela Noack, Tom Schneiter, Winston Atkins, and Margaret Powell at Sterling Memorial Library for their full and gracious support of this undertaking.

In terms of external lenders, the exhibition has benefited immeasurably from the generosity of several collectors. We are deeply grateful to Christopher Forbes and The FORBES Magazine Collection, with its superb holdings by women artists, for their support on numerous levels. Mark Samuels Lasner cheerfully permitted us to invade his amazing library and borrow from it. We are also grateful to Nicolette and Harold Wernick, Suzanne McCormick, Mr. and Mrs. Christopher Forbes, Robert P. Coale, Susan C. Ricci, and Nancy Marshall Strebeigh for lending objects from their private collections, walls, and libraries. Catherine Tedford and the Richard F. Brush Art Gallery and Permanent Collection at St. Lawrence University must also be thanked for kindly lending to this enterprise.

Others shared their time and expertise, including Robyn Asleson, Pamela Gerrish Nunn, and Jan Marsh. Graduate students have also been a part of the process of developing and staging *A Struggle for Fame,* particularly in the graduate seminars on the topic offered by the co-organizers as well as in independent work. We would especially like to single out the diligent labors of Jennifer Stern, Graduate Intern in the Paintings Department, and the research of Nancy Marshall. Without the collective assistance of all these individuals, this exhibition's "struggle for fame" would have been very much impeded and imperiled.

Susan P. Casteras, Curator of Paintings
Linda H. Peterson, Professor of English

From "Safe Havens" to "A Wide Sea of Notoriety"

SUSAN P. CASTERAS

The "struggle for fame" was both a historical reality for women and the title of an 1883 triple-decker novel written by Charlotte Riddell chronicling the fate of an author named Glenarva Westley. While Westley's tribulations were confined to the literary world, many of the prejudices and woes she faced and the anxieties she felt were also shared by her kindred spirits in the realm of art throughout the period of Victoria's long reign (1837–1901). For example, in Westley's arduous progress towards fame, she begins in inexperience and utter ignorance, largely because knowledge of the business world was typically closed to women. Thus, "she did not know how books were printed or published. She had never met an author, she was not acquainted with any person who had ever met one." [1] Despite her naiveté, Westley is driven to write; Riddell even describes her protagonist's inner drive as a dangerous mania that intermittently leaves her troubled, bewildered, and physically exhausted. Westley also feels she must keep her intensely-felt ambitions clandestine, "perfectly aware that even her most modest aspirations would meet with no favour, the young author…in the solitude of her own mind dreamed her fancies, perfected her stories, indulged her hopes, and bore her disappointments." [2] She writes under an assumed name until one of her publishers advertises it widely, thereby unmasking the protective cloak of feminine anonymity. As a result, Westley feels violated and almost undressed, as if she has been reduced to mere

> …common property. Hitherto she had shrunk morbidly from publicity; now she was placed in a strong light for everyone who pleased to stare at and criticize…. Almost to her terror, and certainly to her annoyance…. [she] found people were talking about her by name, and

> that the safe haven of a quiet life was exchanged for that wide sea of notoriety where authors make more enemies than friends. [3]

Westley is also castigated for her choice of subject matter, which her childhood friend, Ned Beattie, asserts her husband should have regulated. He announces that Mr. Lacere should not have "allowed" her to publish her last book and fumes, "if you had been my wife I would have made you burn it." [4] (Indeed, the female author in Mary Cholmondeley's *Red Pottage* of 1899 has her manuscript burned by a man who resents her writing and claims to "know better" how she should spend her time.) Beattie also reiterates the old arguments about suitable themes for women to treat by asking Westley, "why did you not give us a story calculated to make us all happier and brighter and better—a womanly sort of tale about flowers and children and happy lovers?" [5]

Fame, which in her youth Glenarva Westley defined as a fragile bubble, betrays her and her sex at the end, making her a "sinner" mostly because she has seemingly enjoyed too much her period of notoriety in society and has allegedly become prideful as well. Repeatedly Westley is reminded by males to forsake ambition and prestige and return to her socially endorsed, "proper" female role. Beattie pities her spouse, scolding that "it must be hard for your husband…but it serves him right for marrying a clever woman, or rather a woman who is considered clever. When I choose a wife I'll take very good care that if she can read she can't write." [6] Another compatriot from Ireland, Bernard Kelly, remonstrates with equal vociferousness about Westley's prescribed role and believes her husband

> …does right to teach her she is not regarded quite as a prophet at home…. She ought to

stop at home and write her books and mind her house, and see her husband's slippers are warmed, instead of going about to parties and listening to foolish compliments, and frittering away such talents as God has given her in small-talk and company babble.[7]

Even Mr. Lacere, whose pride was vulnerable because Glenarva produced more income than he, "did not want her to write…knew perhaps it would be better for her and happier for him if she never wrote another line…[and] really had not the faintest idea of the power she possessed."[8] Instead of genuine encouragement, he merely indulges her whims, somewhat insidiously cooing, "Remember, dear, that I never wish you to think of publishing except for your own pleasure. Do not trouble yourself now about money or money-making; leave all that to me."[9]

Glenarva Westley Lacere is furthermore chided for not foreseeing the consequences of her ambitions and good fortune and anticipating the ominous time when, after nearly reaching "the highest peak of fame to which she could ever hope to climb…sought after, flattered, caressed, made much of," she would encounter defeat and the devastating statement, "We never even heard of you."[10] Unable to savor her rewards for long, she seems haunted by earlier fears that

…no human being ever believed she was the right person in the right place. Not when she was plodding amongst the London publishers—not when she was making a little money—not when she had gained a great reputation—not when the time came no one could ever deny she had achieved more than nine hundred ninety-nine women out of a thousand ever do achieve—no, not even then did any friend, or relative, or stranger realize it was really Glenarva who had won success, and not some quite independent power associated with her in an unaccountable and uncanny sort of alliance.[11]

Here, too the crux of feminine self-esteem and success is addressed: for even after she attains

transient fame, Westley and her entire sex are deemed unworthy and unable to deal with it and not to have really merited it in the first place. Her struggles, perseverance, and talent seem irrelevant, and her fame more the aberrational result of some phenomenal force that swept her along than a consequence of her abilities.

Westley's ill-fated career raises various salient points and issues to be considered in this essay about the practical realities of a vocation; the inner anxieties and frustrations of women; the exclusivity of male realms of power and the difficulties of access; the bias against earning a living; the impact of marriage; and male definitions of recognition, critical standards, and the art market. For example, Westley pays the psychic cost of carving out a name for herself by bearing scars inflicted by varying blows: lack of encouragement; the humiliation of being intermittently ignored, ridiculed, rejected, and overexposed to the glare of publicity; shame at "abandoning" traditional female roles; and other stresses and strains. She also faces the question of economic self-reliance, since her monetary powers clearly intimidate her spouse and other men.

Another key message conveyed by these fictional experiences is the mixture of conflict, ambivalence, frustration, and guilt that the prospect of fame and its attendant power generated for her and other women. The dynamics of creative inferiority, cultural submissiveness, and general low self-worth were all heady deterrents, making the leap from womanly selflessness to artistic fame a quantum one. The very mythologizing and enshrinement of the woman's sphere kept expectations low; to move beyond middle-class security and the domestic circle to pursue a vocation was daring, and earning a living in the field of art was the province and privilege of men alone.

The issue of male criticism of female work is also germane, not only in terms of how Glenarva Westley reacted, but also how she symbolized the general unpreparedness of Victorian women to deal with critical evaluation of their work. The literary world was overwhelmingly a male enclave, with very few regular female critics in mainstream magazines either in literature or art. Schooled to be overly sensitive and submissive, women were not ready to cope with either extremes of wilting condescension from male critics or their effusive, invariably culturally loaded, praise. The fear of seeming unwomanly, either personally or professionally, was unexpressed yet seemingly omnipresent and, coupled with other factors, left women poorly equipped to confront the politics of criticism and the commerce of art, since they were more culturally attuned to sacrificing for others rather than promoting themselves.

While Glenarva Westley's trials were fictitious, the issue of female experiences and expectations of creativity was very genuine, as were the many hurdles that challenged women in the fine arts. The struggle for fame personified by Riddell's protagonist was decidedly paralleled in real life by the trials, strivings, and achievements of countless female artists during the Victorian era. Although these women only occasionally appear to have left concrete documents (diaries, correspondence, or autobiographies) confirming this, there are nonetheless allusions to their battles in the increasing number of memoirs and reminiscences (e.g., by Henrietta Ward, Lady Butler, and Anna Lea Merritt) especially after the 1880s that underscored, consciously or not, their common challenges as well as their individual gains, usually in remarkably self-deprecating tones.

This exhibition can highlight only a selection of Victorian women artists, deliberately chosen from amateur and professional ranks, who, against considerable odds, created many cultural levels and varieties of art—high, medium, and low, private and commercial, unknown and recognized. It is not the aim to focus merely on those women who, like Glenarva Westley, achieved some degree of fame, although this is true of many of them; instead, a diverse spectrum of efforts and productions of art—from amateur landscape views, private sketchbooks, published and unpublished drawings, commercial illustrations, and full-scale works of art—is explored. Collectively, the range of makers—from anonymity or unappreciated status, to royalty and aristocracy, to middle-class practitioners whose names enjoyed some degree of contemporary recognition—clearly affirms the existence of an important female tradition of making art that flourished in England, despite formidable obstacles, for all of Victoria's reign.

Glenarva Westley might also have wondered, as a late twentieth-century audience does, whether the notion of fame is so culturally encoded in favor of masculine talent that it can serve as an ultimate measure of ability. Current audiences would also debate for different reasons whether women should be perceived as a separate class of creators at all. Whatever the resolution of these arguments, sexual segregation of artists and gendered vision of them and their output certainly existed in the Victorian era ideologically, critically, and institutionally. In this light, the collective labors of women are displayed separately in this venture in order to present the production of art to modern viewers and to allow consideration of the often-hidden history of women artists within the general canon of nineteenth-century art.

Recent revisionist scholars have made commendable progress in unearthing and evaluating the history of women artists in England and in analyzing the forms of discrimination they faced in terms of the selection, judgment, display, and privilege of creating art.[12] As one of the leading historians has indicated, women artists were in actuality quite a frequent and "hot topic in the British world from 1850 to the end of the century, though most convenient histories of the arts in the Victorian age seem reluctant to tell us so."[13] This exhibition provides a partial remedy by offering a selective framework of that same period of history, examining women's different personal circumstances as well as their shared goals, tribulations, subjects, and at times their political beliefs.

Fig. 1 "Female School of Art, Queen Square," *Illustrated London News*, 1868

Starting with an overview of women's art education, this essay will also address social imperatives that influenced the production of art, including cultural biases; institutional advantages and disadvantages; critics, mentors, and patrons; the impact of marriage and motherhood; sisterhood and feminist interconnections; and thematic proclivities. Although a great many women's names could be additionally cited throughout these pages, those of the artists in the exhibition are primarily singled out as relevant examples. Specific basic but brief biographical data, along with fundamental details and numerous reproductions of the objects in this exhibition, are provided in the checklist at the end. By examining women's diverse productions in these arenas, it is possible to study women artists in the context of their peers and to examine how the women represented in the exhibition "A Struggle for Fame" reacted to the daunting variables of exclusion and exclusiveness: criticism, prejudice, institutional obstacles, family circumstances, domestic responsibilities, and other factors.

❦❦❦❦❦❦❦❦❦❦❦❦❦❦❦❦❦❦❦❦❦❦❦

From "Accomplishments" to Art Schools

Constructions of femininity in the Victorian era firmly precluded women from belonging to the category of genius. Men and boys could be geniuses, but women—seen primarily as sensitive, emotional, passive, intuitive, and imitative—were believed capable only of transmitting or nurturing genius in males as wives, mothers, daughters, and sisters.[14] Artistic creativity was not flatly denied about women, but rather redirected or rechanneled into forms of art that emphasized the separate spheres of the sexes—e.g., glorifying to women the innocent pleasures and entertainment value of drawing over the value of producing high art or pursuing a professional vocation.[15] Art for ladies was meant to instill a knowledge of what was beautiful in the world, thereby inculcating a refinement of taste that enhanced social skills appropriate to the activities of the parlor but not to the rigors of the art market. In the eighteenth century, e.g., ladylike accomplishments included dancing, music, and art, and drawing masters were routinely employed to teach women the rudiments of painting and drawing. However, this situation changed in the Victorian period, when a new national art system as well as drawing manuals for the masses supplanted the influence of the drawing master.[16] Artistic "how-to" books, e.g., essentially functioning as drawing masters in print, were often dictatorial and patronizing in tone, telling women how to appreciate, as well as make, art and how to apply the results to the feminine domestic confines of home. While the manuals might encourage step-by-step learning, the final message was clear: women should focus on needlework and painting flowers, shells, still lifes, and landscape views (as Anne Rushout, Mary Darby, Elizabeth Gurney, and Amelia Long did), not attempt figure compositions with complex historical or literary themes; moreover, they should not transcend the boundaries of ladylike accomplishment and invade the commercial and professional sphere.

Authors of these artistic advice books appealed to middle-class ladies, who presumably took to heart the latent messages conveyed in ladies' magazines too. For example, sketching and watercolor were preferable media because they were more "feminine" in nature—neater and easier to conceal, transport, or remain in the background. As *The Lady's Magazine and Museum of Belles Lettres* propagandistically intoned, "Oil painting, for many reasons, will never find superior female professors; there is that sort of squalid discomfort in its pursuit that makes it exceedingly repugnant to elegant women."[17]

Drawing was also deemed a womanly pursuit for reasons enunciated by the famous advice-giver Mrs. Sarah Stickney Ellis, who maintained that this activity reinforced certain desirable feminine traits by being unobtrusive, positive, private, and not deeply intellectual or distracting:

> *It is quiet, it disturbs no one…. It is true, it may when seen offend the practiced eye; but we can always draw in private and keep our productions to ourselves…. [Drawing] is of all other occupations the one most calculated to keep the mind from brooding upon the self, and to maintain that general cheerfulness which is a part of social and domestic duty.*[18]

In terms of more serious art education, Victorian women certainly enjoyed more options than had been available even a few years earlier. As numerous historians have revealed, women at the most powerful bastion of art, the Royal Academy, despite the founding presence in 1763 of Angelica Kauffman and Mary Moser, enjoyed only honorary status as sporadic contributors to the annual exhibitions.[19] (Honorary membership continued well into the twentieth century, when Annie Swynnerton was named an associate member in 1922 and Laura Knight gained full membership in 1936.)

Women were also barred from attending classes at the R.A. until the 1850s. Nonetheless, several touchstone events in this volatile decade were supported by various women represented in this exhibition. The landmark petition of 1859 urging the R.A. to admit women was signed by Emily Osborn, Florence Claxton, Rebecca Solomon, Henrietta Ward, Barbara Smith Bodichon, and Anna Blunden. The next year, Helen Allingham's maternal aunt, Laura Herford, scored another gain when she was accidentally admitted to the R.A. after her sample work (signed only with initials) was accepted. However, the R.A. seemed uncomfortable with this new situation and the "invasion" of even just a few women and imposed a moratorium against admitting more women until the late 1860s. Its reactionary stance was typical of the sluggishness with which reforms and opportunities generally developed and concessions were reluctantly made. Despite the fact (or perhaps partly because of it) that women soon won some top awards (Louisa Starr received the coveted gold medal for history painting in 1867 and Lady Butler won great acclaim), the Academy seemed supremely uneasy with their new female constituency.

Revisionist historical discourses have also reported how the restrictions at the R.A. and elsewhere meant that artistic women had only limited options for art education: to arrange for private tutors, to be instructed by family members or friends, to be largely self-taught (thanks to drawing manuals by Hannah Bolton, B. F. Gandee, John Ruskin, and others), to try to attend one of the government schools of design (intended for working-class artisans, not middle-class matriculants), to study at places like Sass's (later Cary's) or Dickinson's (subsequently Leigh's, then Heatherley's) Academies, or even to move to the continent to work in an atelier.

A Female School of Design opened in 1843, but it was mostly intended for working-class students (not middle-class women) with the goal of improving the level of design for industrial and practical application, especially manufacture, in England. Although lower- and working-class women undoubtedly also produced art, it is largely that of their middle-class, Caucasian counterparts that has survived, a testimony to the way that middle-class women flocked to art education—private, government, or institutionally sponsored—during the Victorian era. In 1857 the School of Design became the National Art Training School at South Kensington and later evolved, after threatened dissolution in 1859, into the Royal Female School of Art (Fig. 1) in 1862, surviving in part due to Queen Victoria's own support of the project. Like other art programs, this one offered competitions and prizes as well as training, including a life class with draped living models, and evening programs.

A signal event in the Victorian era for women was the founding of the Society of Female Artists in 1856–57. In 1857 there had been a strenuous campaign waged to pressure the R.A. to admit women students, and this was actively supported by, among others, Henrietta Ward and Barbara Smith Bodichon. *The English Woman's Journal,* another reform spearheaded by Smith Bodichon, editorialized in 1858 that any comparisons with other institutions was unjust and "…wholly irrelevant so long as the domestic and academical facilities afforded to the female artist are so very far below those of a male student."[20] As has been summarized, reactions to this new institution ran "the gamut of attitudes, from suspicion and anger at female autonomy, through patronising or amused tolerance, to a double-edged support for female segregation which amounted to banishment from other venues."[21]

One of the best things about the Society was that it gave women a clear-cut chance to shape, supervise, and professionalize their own institution.[22] In 1863 it opened its own school and remained in operation beyond the end of Victoria's reign, sporadically changing its name to the Society of Lady Artists in 1872 and the Society of Women Artists in 1899. At its inaugural show and the following one, works by Ward, Smith Bodichon, Anna Howitt, and Blunden were all on view. Later contributors or honorary members included Florence Claxton, Rebecca Solomon, Jessica Landseer, Lady Butler, and Mary Ellen Edwards; Lady Waterford also was involved with its reorganization efforts in 1865. In response to the accusation that too many amateurs were flooding this venue and decreasing the quality of its exhibitions, the Society in time mandated that only professional artists could be members and that amateurs had to pay fees to exhibit works. In some ways the Society fell prey to its single-sex status, being vulnerable to erratic criticism from both sexes and also to the economic reality that it was more important to have works shown at the Royal Academy and elsewhere than a "lowly" women's venue. However, despite the vicissitudes of the press, fluctuating numbers of contributors, and a dearth of consistent support from established women artists after they "made" their names, the Society did much to improve the lot of women. As *The Art Journal* affirmed about one of its greatest accomplishments, simply giving women a visual forum, "There are among these pictures productions of a quality so rare, as at once to achieve a reputation for their authors, yet which, but for the establishment of a society of lady artists, had never been seen."[23]

The issue of access to nude models by women artists was also central to the structuring of artistic education as well as a controversial topic throughout the period in virtually all programs of instruction.[24] Women were not permitted to study from the nude at the Royal Academy until 1903 and then only in a separate class; there had been an optional course in 1892 for women to study from draped living models, but the latter were so swathed in protective wrapping as to have made the opportunity rather comic. In general, women often solved this problem on their own by hiring models and arranging for special classes conducted elsewhere and at alternative times. By contrast, other schools were more innovative on this front; at Leigh's Academy classes from the nude were part of the curriculum, as were women's anatomy classes and year-round instruction. Hailed as "the first school to admit lady students on equal terms with men," Leigh's had low fees and attracted such women students as Laura Herford, Louise Jopling, and Anna Blunden.[25]

There were other alternatives like the Society of British Artists, which in 1846 opened an art school with life classes for women, and a few years later Queen's College, Bedford College for Women, and Ladies College similarly opened their doors just for women. These institutions also offered some drawing classes in their curricula, and Smith Bodichon was among the women who went to lectures at one of these colleges. In 1859 the Crystal Palace School of Art was founded and incorporated nude classes into its program; later it boasted Eleanor Fortescue Brickdale as one of its distinguished alumnae. The Slade School of Art was also unusual, admitting women from its beginning in 1871, although initially providing only separate classes for the study of living draped models. Numerous women attended and won prizes there, among them Kate Greenaway and Evelyn Pickering DeMorgan.

Art schools also empowered women to become potential teachers, and this was the case with numerous artists who served on existing faculties or adventurously opened their own schools or tutelage systems. In this respect Henrietta Ward was a trailblazer, opening her own program in 1879, while Emily Osborn taught at the Norwich School of Art, Eleanor Fortescue Brickdale at Byam Shaw's school, and Annie French at the Glasgow School of Art. The art school environment informed and clarified for women the process by which males climbed the proverbial ladder of success. In doing so, women could profit by learning about the stages and strategies required to receive awards and be featured in solo exhibitions. At least a few women reached this rung of the ladder: Smith Bodichon had three of her works exhibited on their own in 1858 and others at Pall Mall and the French Gallery in 1859 and 1861, respectively; Lady Butler earned one-woman shows at the Fine Art Society in 1877 and 1881, while Emily Osborn had a similar arrangement at Goupil's in 1886. The Fine Art Society also championed Helen Allingham and Kate Greenaway, the former with shows in 1887, 1889, 1891, 1894, and 1898 and the latter with solo displays in 1894 and 1898. Eleanor Fortescue Brickdale, like Evelyn Pickering DeMorgan, was the subject of various full-length articles and a solo exhibition in London; she had her own work on display at the Dowdeswell Gallery in 1901 and at Leigh House the following year.[26]

Cultural Captives

When women contended on the same training turf with men and abjured domestic domains to mix with male classmates, the results were often quite revealing. George Dunlop Leslie, a conservative artist writing in 1914 about the inner life of the Royal Academy during the reign of Queen Victoria, provided illuminating yet depressing insight into the double (if not multiple) bind that encumbered female artists in alien masculine territory: they had to act like ladies, not equals, yet were treated more like docile pets than serious students:

> The girls, it must be confessed, worked very hard and well; numbers of them have taken medals over the heads of the boys, especially in later years. They are more attentive to the teaching of the Visitors than the generality of the boys, though, for the most part, they lack the self-reliant conceit that so often characterises the brightest geniuses of the male sex....[27]

After identifying the low self-esteem of women, Leslie then inadvertently confesses his sexist attitudes (and later his colleagues' ageist biases) and preference for instructing only young and pretty females:

> It is very pleasant work teaching girls, especially pretty ones, who somehow always seemed to me to make the best studies. Possibly I may have been biassed in their favour, for all my life I have regarded good-looking girls with feelings of gratitude; but it is certainly remarkable that, as a general rule, the prettier the girl the better the study. Girls are very receptive of careful coaching, and it may be that a pretty girl, as she passes through her art training, when the teachers are men, receives decidedly more attention than falls to the lot of her plainer companions; it is not quite fair, but I am afraid it is inevitable.[28]

Masculine biases pervaded other areas with equal strength. Just as the publishing world had been a conundrum to Glenarva Westley, so too was the art world a forbidden and mysterious masculine entity to Victorian women artists. Since women were very rarely art dealers, curators, or judges on important art juries in the contemporary art world, they had little access to authority (except in the rarefied confines of the Society of Female Arts). In this regard the marginalization of women was perhaps most injurious and severe, since concomitant with their exclusion from the exercise of power were the cultural imperatives about the feminine sphere of influence. This left women afraid of appearing non-conformist, of risking their reputations, of offending their families, and of suffering the insult of "unwomanliness." (See Fig. 2 for *Punch*'s lampoon of female artists.)

Women needed male critics as much as their male counterparts did, for their attention, guidance, and access to audiences, galleries, collectors, and dealers; arguably they may have needed them even more, since it was unacceptable for women to be aggressive and seek out patrons, dealers, or publicity.[29] Unless supported by a male critic (few women held this powerful position), women artists and their prospects were extremely limited and doomed. The vast masculine art world of privilege was intimidating and overwhelming, while its converse, the female theatre of influence, was circumscribed and powerless.

Yet women were consumers as well as makers of art, although their roles were typically trivialized and underplayed; certainly they went to see art and may have been part of the decision-making process about buying art and placing it in their homes. As spectators of art they were also vulnerable to attack and were, in effect, taught to see differently, both life in general and art, including women's art. They were instructed to rely on male criticism as a gauge of their ability and discouraged from competing with men for prizes and commissions. Women were urged to keep their gaze averted in social contact and, symbolically, in art as well, especially from seeing the nude. Although they were frequent visitors to the Royal Academy exhibitions and galleries, even this activity was gendered. The act of looking at art seemed exclusively male to many; thus, the motives imputed for feminine vision or consumption of art were ridiculed in many ways, e.g., by a writer who damns a female visitor to the Royal Academy exhibition for merely "scribbling her criticism on the margin of the catalogue, doubtless for the benefit of some aftercomer whom she wishes to impress with respect to her discriminating powers in Art."[30] In countless paintings, literary descriptions, and *Punch* cartoons, it is the women who are made to gaze superficially at art, while men look seriously at pictures, unless they have been distracted by attractive females on whom they gaze instead. This situation is lampooned, e.g., in an 1867 issue of *London Society* (Fig. 3) to which Adelaide

Claxton contributed an illustration. Her female spectators are made fun of as "dainty academy belles," not serious art students, connoisseurs, or collectors. Accordingly, the accompanying doggerel dismisses their shallow frivolity: "In pictures of children they revel—/ Call Hayllar a duck and a dear, / And Millais (when down to their level)/ The pet of all painters this year.... / Of harmony, colour, and keeping / They're ignorant—joking apart; / And a picture of Baby sleeping / They think is the highest of Art."[31]

Fig. 2 Arthur Hopkins, "A Vocation Missed," *Punch,* 1897

A VOCATION MISSED.

Mr. Brown. "LOOK HERE, MARIA. LOOK AT THE YOUNG LADY'S LIGHT TOUCH!"
Mrs. Brown. "EH! WHAT A HAND FOR PASTRY!!"

Critics, Mentors, & Patrons

The saga of exclusiveness and exclusion continued in these areas as well, with a gendered differential or vision of art shared by critics, artists, and audiences alike, making the sex of a creator more important than any other element such as artistic background or innate talent. In life class part of the issue had been a woman's right to look at the nude and portray it; in the art world a woman's painting had to be defended for its right to exist and be considered in the context of men's contributions. Victorian males surveyed, ordered, and controlled the art world and the "rightful gaze," and constantly offered women prescriptive lectures and counsel on their limited place as outsiders in the art world. Some women

Fig. 3 Adelaide Claxton, "Academy Belles," *London Society*, 1867

ACADEMY BELLES.

undoubtedly protested, but collectively they were not rebellious very often and did not successfully revolt in sufficient numbers until the advent of the suffragette movement. In 1901 this was as true as it had been fifty years earlier, as the comments of Walter Shaw Sparrow (who wrote *Women Painters of the World* in 1905) attest. In an article for *The Studio* about Eleanor Fortescue Brickdale, he resurrects the prevailing beliefs about women's creativity and worries if women become masculinized in their quest for fame and honors. Upholding the validity of separate spheres, he deceptively compliments Fortescue Brickdale as "a lady of real genius."[32] Given her gifts, however, he muses, "should a woman of genius make herself the imitative slave of men-artists and their ways of work" or should she be satisfied with her supposedly great gifts of intuition?[33] By imitating male styles or success, she may perilously risk "developing the masculine traits of her genius at the expense of the feminine."[34] Sparrow admits, however, that "there is at the present time very little recognition for any lady of artistic genius who does not aim at becoming *un homme manqué*."[35] To him such a woman/incomplete man could merely produce a pale imitation of masculine ability and be only a second-class, "gracious daughter of what men have achieved...."[36] He also circuitously argues that, although "these true and generous women-artists wait for a just recognition" and "stand in need of pen-knights," he personally believes that "what the world needs now is a general return to womanliness by the ladies who try to be artists."[37]

Turning their gender against them in often specious yet chivalrous terms, Sparrow admits that men are flattered to be imitated yet hypocritical in their double standard of thinking:

> *if they can say of a woman's work in art that it is a* tour de force, *'almost bold enough to be a man's, you know,' they put on a ludicrous air of mingled pride and condescension; but when a work is a Lady Waterford's, instinct with womanly grace, fancy, waywardness,*

tenderness, and intuition, they marvel, more often than not, why anyone should speak of it enthusiastically, as though its limitations were not clear for all folk to see.[38] Overall, however, this critic enunciated the conventional biased judgment that masculine art was always superior and that "the highest praise that can be given to a sister of art is to say that her genius grows in strength without losing its womanliness."[39]

As Sparrow's comments indicate, the unique and separate qualities of male and female art were, even as a new century dawned, still endorsed by most critics. Accordingly, polarities of sexual/artistic characteristics were upheld and reiterated ad nauseam—e.g., women's art was seen as typically delicate, charming, weak, pretty, sweet, retiring, and derivative, while men's productions were bold, forceful, strong, penetrating, vigorous, and innovative. At times some women broke through the gender barrier of criticism and were singled out and praised for the allegedly masculine qualities of their art. This was notably the case for Henrietta Ward, Emily Osborn, Rebecca Solomon, and Lady Butler. Ward, one of the most celebrated female artists of the 1850s and 1860s, did not have her work hailed for masculine traits; instead her work was sexually categorized and continually compared with that of her husband, fellow artist Edward Matthew Ward. Osborn, on the other hand, had her historical picture *The Escape of Lord Nithisdale from the Tower,* displayed at the 1861 Royal Academy exhibition, complimented precisely because:

the subject…is a bold one for a lady, and she has treated it with more strength and historical power than are usually ascribed to her sex. Some of the artistic lords of the creation, who succeed in treating such subjects with great feebleness, must begin to feel rather jealous, as they certainly ought to feel very much humbled, at being outstripped in their professional race.[40]

Similarly, Solomon's *Peg Woffington's Visit to Triplet* (Fig. 4) from the prior Academy show elicited the sexist compliment that this "is really a picture of great power, and in execution so firm and masculine that it would scarcely be pronounced the work of a lady…. It is gratifying, encouraging, and full of hope, to find a picture so admirably painted by a lady…."[41]

Perhaps the most commanding example in this category is Elizabeth Thompson (Lady Butler), who enjoyed a meteoric rise to fame when her "masculine" military subject of *The Roll Call* at the 1874 Royal Academy exhibition caused a sensation in the press and with the public. Amazement was continually registered that a woman could execute such a "virile" image of stoic male suffering; critics acknowledged she had successfully invaded a male field and eternally phrased this feat in masculine terms. *The Spectator* applauded the "thoroughly manly point of view," while *The Times* condescendingly concurred that "there is no sign of a woman's weakness."[42] Besides going on nationwide tour and being mobbed by astonished admirers, the popular painting triggered the unprecedented nomination of its artist as a potential member of the Royal Academy. While this attempt did not succeed, it nonetheless underscored how crucial masculine support—as well as supposed masculine qualities in her art—were in a woman artist's struggle for recognition and prestige.

Probably the most influential critic of the period for both men and women was John Ruskin, whose relationship with female artists was often sympathetic, although his dictatorial style was basically patriarchal and controlling. He dispensed advice to all classes of women, not just middle- and upper-class ladies, and seemingly preferred the untutored ones most in need and in awe of his often overbearing counsel. Certainly his interaction with Elizabeth Siddal, Anna Blunden, Lady Waterford, Francesca Alexander, Kate Greenaway, Anna Howitt, and Lady Butler all had a personal and/or critical impact on them. Siddal,

Fig. 4 W. Thomas engraving after Rebecca Solomon, "Peg Woffington's Visit to Triplet," *Illustrated London News*, 1867

e.g., received Ruskin's emotional and financial support; he pronounced her a genius and offered her (with various strings attached) a generous yearly stipend that she chose to reject in 1857. Remarkably enough, she resisted his interference and must have tired of his tedious, endless recommendations, e.g., that she cease making "fancies" or imaginary scenes like *The Woeful Victory* and instead turn to more mundane themes drawn from real things in a plainer, duller fashion.[43] A different type of relationship existed with Lady Waterford, a wealthy woman of elite station whom Ruskin nonetheless scolded constantly about her art. He even commented on the tensions between her status as aristocratic lady and painter, stating:

> as for the good which you might do by actual painting, this also depends wholly on the position you are willing to take. If you think it would not be right that a marchioness should be a good artist, if there is any feeling which would keep you from making the art a main object,…then your work never will be good for much except to show that your principles of judgement are right and true.[44]

Despite his nagging, to the end of her correspondence with him Lady Waterford strictly retained the willing role of pupil to mentor, enduring Ruskin's barbs and harangues yet respecting his intellectual abilities.

Anna Blunden's background, by contrast, was far from privileged, and she was forced to earn a living as a governess before being inspired by Ruskin's *Modern Painters* to seek a career in art. Her relationship with Ruskin was more one-sided, particularly because she chose to adore and pursue him with obnoxious persistence. Yet he did not abandon their correspondence, presumably since the desire to instruct and influence such an admiring female was too strong a temptation. He also delivered to her some of his most scathing remarks about women artists: "That is the worst of you women," he exploded, "you are always working to your feelings and never to plain purposes. If you cannot draw for drawing's sake, and wouldn't draw if you were alone in the world, you will *never* draw."[45] He complained:

> *As far as I know lady painters ALWAYS let their feelings run away with them, and get to painting angels and mourners when they should be painting brickbats and stones. If you were my pupil,…and a youth instead of a young lady, I should at once forbid all senti-ment for a couple of years, and set you to paint, first—a plain white cambric pocket handkerchief—or linen napkin….*[46]

Contrastingly, a much cherished student and welcome confidante was Francesca Alexander, whose talent for delineating flowers and peasant scenes Ruskin "discovered" and then subsequently published and publicized. He loved the purity of line and spirit embodied by her work and likened its innocence to that of girlishness itself, a likely extension of his own pedophilic worship of innocent females. Alexander's drawings were thus perfect analogues to his own aesthetic and personal tenets, showing humility and devotion in both subject and technique.

With Lady Butler he reversed his standing opinion that women could never be geniuses, although his initial reactions to her potential were tentatively approving but cautionary. It was her 1875 painting *Quatre Bras* which "converted" him into a strong supporter and caused him to glowingly extol its Amazonian virtues:

> *I never approached a picture with more iniquitous prejudice against it than I did Miss Thompson's; partly because I have always said that no woman could paint; and secondly, because I thought what the public made such a fuss about must be good for nothing. But it is amazon's work this; no doubt about it, and the first fine Pre-Raphaelite picture of battle we have had…it remains only for me to make this tardy genuflexion…before this Pallas of Pall Mall….*[47]

Helen Allingham also received accolades from Ruskin, who tried with her as well to have his critical remarks guide her career. Yet while she appreciated his interest, to her credit she did not indulge in heartrending or detailed corres-pondence with him and ultimately preferred to ignore his suggestions and paint things in her own way. By contrast to this rather self-reliant stance was the response of her friend Kate Greenaway. Like Alexander, Greenaway was in some ways basically "undiscovered" (or not very visible) until Ruskin became an eloquent devotee of hers in his typically intense fashion and promoted her talent extensively in his Slade lectures at Oxford and otherwise. Even more than Alexander, Greenaway and Ruskin shared a close relationship and wrote over a thousand letters, his quasi-chivalric, patriarchal devotion returned with enthusiasm and loyalty by Greenaway's friendship and discipleship. Unlike Allingham and certain others, Greenaway eagerly accepted Ruskin's critical guidance and venerated his opinion and mentorship.

Yet the archetypal critic of the period could also traumatize women artists. Ruskin's words apparently broke the spirit of Anna Howitt, whose mother claimed his "severe private censure of one of her oil paintings so crushed her sensitive nature as to make her yield to her bias for the super-natural and withdraw from the ordinary arena of the fine arts."[48] Ironically, a few years earlier Howitt seemingly dedicated her book, *An Art Student in Munich,* to Ruskin, a testimony at the time to his influence upon her and presumably upon other women students. Her regrettable situation was extreme but perhaps not rare, although over the years Ruskin seems to have mellowed somewhat in his attitudes about women artists. In general, while he did a disservice to many of them, he opened some doors, at least partly, for others and even occasionally unlocked the minds and eyes of Victorian audiences to art executed by the so-called inferior sex.

Beyond the question of acceptance or rejection, as has been pointed out, for female artists "producing work was the first struggle, exhibiting it the second, and selling it the third. The last two stages of success involved both luck and judgement."[49] In this respect women scored some recorded successes, along with the inevitable failures, although research on this topic continues to emerge and provide a fuller assessment of the situation. For some women, selling their art was clearly not an option at all; art was a private endeavor, and incursions into commercial transactions were forbidden by family or personal dictate. Others permitted their art to be sold or marketed for purely eleemosynary purposes; e.g., the Princess Royal contributed an etching for an auction to help raise money for "the Patriotic Fund at the time of the Crimean War," while Francesca Alexander's pen-and-ink drawings of Tuscany were sold to benefit local charities.[50] In a similarly magnanimous gesture, Lady Waterford executed a series of frescoes with mostly biblical themes for a Northumberland village school.

Some women enjoyed a degree of patronage from male buyers; Howitt had Thomas Fairbairn, a supporter of the Pre-Raphaelites, purchase her 1855 work *The Castaways,* and Boyce's *Outcast* was bought by another Pre-Raphaelite patron, Thomas Plint.[51] While Blunden's *God's Gothic* was purchased by the artist David Roberts, Siddal (besides receiving Ruskin's monetary support) sold *Clerk Saunders* to Charles Eliot Norton. Men such as Charles Mitchell (who bought *Pickles and Preserves*) and his brother (who commissioned a portrait of the Sturgis family) were customers of Osborn, and Charles Prater purchased Rebecca Solomon's *Peg Woffington* canvas. Eleanor Fortescue Brickdale also fared well, selling virtually all the works from a 1901 solo show at Dowdeswell Gallery in London.

There was also the phenomenon of what has been described as "matronage," or female clients for works of art.[52] Queen Victoria, who bought the original version of Osborn's *The Governess* as well as *My Cottage Door,* commissioned portraits of some of her offspring from Henrietta Ward and also bought Lady Butler's *The Roll Call* and commissioned *The Defense of Rorke's Drift* from her. Osborn was moreover fortunate to have Lady Chetwynd buy her signal work, *Nameless and Friendless,* while *The Illustrated London News* bought and published another work in 1862. Barbara Smith Bodichon was not only an artist but also a "matron" of the arts, commissioning a portrait of herself from Osborn for Girton College. Another prominent philanthropist, Angela Burdett-Coutts, purchased Solomon's 1858 *Behind the Curtain.* Merritt and Allingham also had several female purchasers of their pictures, and unknown numbers of women bought books illustrated by Fortescue Brickdale, Greenaway, and other artists.

On a larger scale, the Fine Art Society furthered the careers and capitalized on the successes of a trio of eminent women—Lady Butler, Allingham, and Greenaway—earning money for all concerned. Some women even managed to have their art infrequently sold to museums—e.g., Merritt's *Love Locked Out* was bought by the Chantry Bequest, Sophie Anderson's *Elaine* went to Liverpool, and Osborn, Butler, and Allingham enjoyed the distinction of knowing some of their works entered either municipal or royal collections during their lifetimes. Marie Spartali Stillman's *Madonna Pietra* was purchased by the Liverpool Art Gallery in 1884.

Support Groups

Most of the women represented in this exhibition benefited from some form of art classes at one of the institutions previously mentioned. It is furthermore evident that another critical element shared by most of these women (and others) was encouragement or support from family members above all.[53] Anna Howitt's parents were both authors who permitted their daughters to live on their own abroad to study art, while Ward came from a long line of artists. Helen Paterson Allingham's abilities were acknowledged by her maternal aunts, who arranged for her to matriculate at the Birmington School of Design; she also lived with a trailblazing artistic aunt in London when she went to study there. In some cases it was the mother (usually an amateur or aspiring artist) who inspired the daughter, as was true with Osborn (whose mother's artistic dreams were thwarted), Eleanor Vere Boyle (whose mother was a flower painter), Beatrix Potter (whose mother was a watercolorist), Anna Blunden (whose mother apparently painted), and Lady Butler (whose mother and sister were both gifted). In other instances it was the father who played a prominent role: e.g., Joanna Boyce's father escorted her to all-male lectures and functions, and Smith Bodichon's liberal family gave all the daughters art lessons and granted financial independence to her at age twenty-one. Many women had fathers, brothers, or male relatives who were artists—notably Boyce, Solomon, Greenaway, the Hayllar sisters, Potter, Merritt, Ward, Sandys, DeMorgan, and the Claxtons. Some received the benefit of their male relations' training and connections in the commercial world, as well as their moral support.

Others felt the lash of parental opposition—Osborn's curate father was initially reluctant to permit his daughter to go to art school, while Blunden's mother and father wanted her to reconsider returning to the regular employment of being a governess. The only other woman to have earned a living in another field before turning to art was Elizabeth Siddal, whose working-class parents had no money or connections to help their daughter enter the art world; as has been noted, "instead of taking lessons from a drawing master, she became a model" and thereafter pursued art studies.[54] Mary Ellen Edwards' artistic inclinations were seriously dampened by family members until a family friend gave her the necessary tools when she was twelve.[55] Similarly, Evelyn Pickering DeMorgan had an artist uncle whose influence was significant, especially since her affluent and liberal parents resisted allowing her to study art or go to the Slade School. Although relatives on her maternal side were artistic, Pickering's mother was dismayed by her ambitions and bitterly complained, "I want a daughter, not an artist!"[56] Her family even bribed the drawing master to tell their daughter she had no talent, and when he had her work only on still lifes, Pickering rebelled by defiantly drawing a male nude study, an act which shocked her instructor and prompted him to resign his position. Although by age twenty-one she had her own studio, earlier she chafed at the enforced idleness of her life and its ballroom society expectations of her and instead preferred to lock herself into her room to work. She even went alone to live and study in Rome in the 1870s, much as Mary Ellen Edwards proceeded on her own to London.

Another important form of support came from the interlocking network of friendship, acquaintance, and mutual interests that existed at various levels among middle- and upper-class women particularly. When painters, like their literary sisters, personally knew one another, they could presumably discuss and support their mutual efforts and goals. They may have also competed, of course, but this too would have been part of a healthy interchange and opportunity for women who were otherwise deemed culturally aberrant. When the surroundings were dominated by women, as in art classes or partly at the offices of *The English Woman's Journal* and other women's periodicals, male interference was less likely to prevail, and women could conceivably voice their opinions and exert some authority as decisionmakers.

There was some degree of female solidarity or sisterhood latent in this invisible/visible subculture of women, especially in terms of collaborative projects that proliferated among authors, artists, publishers, and family members —evidence of further supportiveness at professional as well as personal levels. Journals like *Judy* and *London Society* seemed to employ numerous women, not only the Claxtons but also Allingham and Edwards as illustrators. Allingham was also commissioned to illustrate a novel by her sister-in-law Anne Thackeray for *Cornhill Magazine;* she was lifelong friends with George Eliot (who asked her to illustrate one of her works) and Ellen Terry (whom Violet Lindsay depicted in her portrait and Anna Lea Merritt also etched in portrait form). While still single, Allingham achieved the almost revolutionary feat of being hired as the sole woman to serve on the staff of *The Graphic,* for which she produced illustrations and read novels by women authors like Mrs. Oliphant.[57]

In terms of the the alliances of friendship, many of the women represented in this exhibition enjoyed intermingling ties. Howitt knew Smith Bodichon, Boyce, and Siddal as well as authors like Mrs. Gaskell and wrote of her personal dream of realizing female solidarity in the form of a utopian women's college of art.[58] Smith Bodichon, the cousin of another crusader, Florence Nightingale, was a friend of Harriet Martineau, Anna Jameson, and the feminist Bessie Rayner Parkes and also knew authors like Christina Rossetti; furthermore, she helped establish not only *The English Woman's Journal* but also the Portfolio Club for artists in 1853–54. She and Howitt produced pencil portraits of Siddal at Smith Bodichon's country house in Scalands and contributed unknown solace to their companion, who was unhappy in her career and in her relationship with Dante Gabriel Rossetti. Siddal also knew Joanna Boyce and wrote to Rossetti about the tragic death of her friend. Allingham enjoyed strong matrilineal precedent in the talents of female relatives like Mrs. Gaskell and Bessie Rayner Parkes; moreover, Allingham met Kate Greenaway during their time at the Slade, and they worked together in the 1880s as fellow neighbors and artists. Generational bonds were also cemented; Eleanor Vere Boyle, the younger cousin of Lady Waterford, received a letter from the latter in 1880 that underscored her perspective on the changing art scene for current women artists: "I get rather dispirited at my failures, and the want of that knowledge and finish I see in all women's work at exhibitions when they have had good training; there was none in my day...."[59]

There were literally creative sisterhoods as well, exemplified by the Hayllar siblings, Lady Butler and her poet sister Alice Meynell, Florence and Adelaide Claxton, Esther Faithfull Fleet and Emily Faithfull (a rare woman publisher), and collaborations struck by individuals like Jessie Macleod and the unidentified "Mary Elizabeth" for the books *Dreamland* and *Fifteen Designs Illustrating Tears.* Moreover, a metaphorical form of sisterhood was undoubtedly fostered by memberships in the same organizations—in this respect, the importance of belonging to groups or clubs and having art school affiliations should not be underestimated. Overall, these friendly, even sisterly, contacts forged a network of acquaintance and reinforced a sense of artistic identity that must have been of inestimable worth, significance, and influence.

Furthermore, there were political interconnections linking some lives. Howitt and Smith Bodichon knew one another and, with Ward, Osborn, and others, shared a commitment to the principle of women artists' rights when they signed a special petition urging admission to the Royal Academy in 1859. Ward, although not a self-proclaimed feminist, lived her principles by tenaciously carving out a career despite domestic difficulties, eight children, and widowhood. Contrastingly, Smith Bodichon lived a life of considerable independence and maintained feminist beliefs throughout her life, helping to organize the Married Women's Property Campaign in 1857, among other reform crusades. While her colleagues Ward, Osborn, Lady Butler, and Allingham were perhaps not overt feminists, they too, years later in 1889 and 1897, were signatories in another document in favor or women's suffrage.

ᴥᴥᴥᴥᴥᴥᴥᴥᴥᴥᴥᴥᴥᴥᴥᴥᴥᴥᴥᴥᴥᴥ

Marriage, Motherhood, and Collaborative Partnerships

Because of their mostly middle- or upper-class backgrounds, the majority of women represented in this exhibition were married at some point, thereby fulfilling societal expectations of the so-called "gentler" and "inferior" sex. The issue of marriage, irrelevant in other discussions, is valid in this context because of its impact on individual creativity and output. It would be a misstatement to say that marriage unequivocally ended a woman's career; while the demands of being a wife and mother in particular taxed feminine energies, there were certainly many instances in which women artists were able to surmount formidable obstacles to create art and contribute to the family income and, in widowhood, to serve as sole breadwinner.

It is clear that some marriages flourished while others undoubtedly faltered under these creative conditions. For Smith Bodichon, who was from the outset individualistic, headstrong, and defiant of convention, this was true even on her honeymoon trip in 1857 to the United States (where she and her husband were fascinated by slavery, feminist leaders like Lucretia Mott, and class structure). While she painted and produced her Louisiana sketchbook and other journals, her French physician spouse enacted a role reversal and shopped, cooked, and cleaned in an obviously unusual and egalitarian relationship.[60] Later the two divided the year between France or Algeria and England, allowing each to pursue separate interests. Marriage did not impede Smith Bodichon's reform efforts, which were always on behalf of women and higher education, whether Girton College, her funding of *The English Woman's Journal,* her writings in *Women and Work* and elsewhere, her arrangements of private exhibitions of art, or her labors on behalf of female suffrage in 1873 and later.

Henrietta Ward fared less well, for although there were separate studios and schedules for her and her artist husband, it was obvious that duties of the household, supervision of servants, and the needs and crises of eight children devolved upon her shoulders, not his. In retrospect, he seems to have benefited more from the arrangement, but at least "in turn her practice was supported by a companionate marriage and shared enterprise."[61]

Joanna Boyce, like Smith Bodichon, had a strong sense of personal identity and expressed in writing her need for autonomy and her misgivings about marriage.[62] Knowledgeable about contemporary literature by and about women, she wed a fellow artist, Henry Wells, in 1857 and managed to produce art on a fairly regular basis. She must have had a cooperative arrangement in art with Wells since, after she died, Siddal sadly wrote to Rossetti, "It will be a fearful blow to her husband for she must have been the head of the firm and most useful to him."[63] Her death after complications of childbirth serves as a grim reminder of the fatal risks Victorian women faced in their roles as mothers and nurturers.

There were also limited partnerships and co-wage-earning situations that existed between Sophie Anderson and her artist husband and to a certain extent between Siddal and Rossetti (who had hoped, e.g., to work together on illustrating ballads compiled by William Allingham).[64] For Evelyn DeMorgan this was particularly true, and it has been said that her marriage to the ceramicist William DeMorgan was "perceived as a perfect partnership between two unworldly artists whose regard for commerce was notoriously subdued to the demands of art."[65] Nonetheless, DeMorgan's capital was crucial to her husband's pottery enterprise, as were her earnings to their dual income. Marie Spartali Stillman, who knew Pickering DeMorgan as well as May Morris, also worked partly to buttress the somewhat erratic family finances, sharing the load with her journalist husband.

Other women made a living from their art not only during marriage, but also before and, when applicable, after widowhood or divorce. This was true of Helen Allingham, who while still an art student helped her widowed mother by doing illustrations for magazines like *Once A Week;* after her own spouse died, Allingham reorganized her life as a productive watercolorist, working six days a week to provide for her six children. Also in this category were Ward, Howitt, Blunden, Boyle, the Claxtons, Edith and Mary Hayllar, Merritt, Lady Butler, Beatrix Potter, Spartali Stillman, and May Morris, the latter revolutionizing embroidering and elevating it from the realm of girlhood decorativeness to the spheres of higher art. Lady Waterford was also widowed but did not have financial worries; by contrast, others like Osborn, Solomon, Greenaway, and Fortescue Brickdale remained single and out of necessity had to support themselves, sometimes enduring considerable hardship.

Thus, those who "made it" as artists were as likely to be married as single, and there seems to be no measurable correlation between whether or not their motherhood or childlessness affected their output. As Ward's and Allingham's personal lives attest, these women were often very resourceful in their juggling of roles. Resourcefulness was also a characteristic of Anderson, who lived in very different places (France, America, England, and the Isle of Capri) and was forced, as well as capable enough, to adapt her production and career to each move. Spartali Stillman also managed to produce, exhibit, and sell art while she lived abroad in Italy.

꧁꧂꧁꧂꧁꧂꧁꧂꧁꧂꧁꧂꧁꧂꧁꧂꧁꧂꧁꧂꧁꧂

On the Subjects of Women

The complexity, richness, and breadth of subjects treated by so many women artists would entail many chapters and analyses that are unfortunately beyond the scope of this essay. Overall, as various modern scholars have pointed out, English women artists tended to produce themes drawn from or related to middle-class life—especially courtship and love, motherhood, church and charitable activities, customs, reverie, leisure pursuits, local scenery, and the Victorian home, especially the parlor and nursery.[66] The subjects were not all rosy; there was also a potentially darker side manifested in the choice to depict workers—notably governesses, sempstresses, milliners, servants, performers, peasants, and even prostitutes. To this a wide cross-section of literary and mythological or imaginary themes, many with female heroines or protagonsts, must be added. Many were influenced stylistically and thematically by men's paintings, although this was true of male artists too, for both sexes reinforced their own culture-bound stereotypes. It cannot thus be expected that women defied the artistic establishment any more than men and produced radically subversive or negative images challenging the status quo or championing strongly feminist subjects. Indeed, this was rarely the case, not only among women but also men, who vied for attention and patronage in the art world by generally appealing to middle-class taste and not reform spirit. Rather than being perceived as a weakness, tendencies toward iconological conformity must be understood in the context of women's restricted place in society. Since women had no control over how images were chosen or achieved popularity, much less how they were

What Tomkins said to Jones—
" BOTHER the old masters, look
at the young Miss-esses."

Fig. 5 Florence Claxton, detail of a page
from *The Adventures of a Woman
in Search of Her Rights*, 1871

bought, reproduced, or circulated, their typical conservatism of theme, more than being a sign of simple compliance or timidity, should be viewed also as a byproduct of female inbred servility to male authority and of women's insecurity in the art world.

Although in the eighteenth century landscape views were popular fare for women artists, this category of art was somewhat less common among Victorian practitioners.[67] Rushout, Long, Darby, and Gurney seem to belong to this earlier tradition and recorded the pleasures of travel and the joy of working outdoors. Traveling and producing landscapes were signs of leisure (e.g., Osborn went as far as North Africa while DeMorgan and Solomon went to the continent), but above all it was the variety and loveliness of the English countryside that imaginatively captivated Mary Hayllar, Landseer, and countless others. Anderson, Osborn, and Boyce also produced landscapes, although their portraits and genre pictures were seemingly much more marketable. The liberation of solitary sketching and painting was also personified by Smith Bodichon, who enjoyed her independent travels to Hastings, Algeria, and elsewhere and immersed herself into capturing the myriad sights she saw. Some women also embraced country life as an artistic vehicle for expression, both personally and professionally; Greenaway preferred the country-side, and Allingham liked her rural retreat and the chance to work *en plein air* in spring and summer months.[68] For Allingham, capitalizing on the public nostalgia for the "pure", unchanging countryside meant using this retardataire association as a marketing tool to produce landscapes that evoked idyllic rural scenes and manufactured picturesqueness to please the eye, soothe the social conscience, and appeal to buyers.

Another aspect of nature was indebted to Ruskinian and Pre-Raphaelite influences and focused on the importance of one-to-one, direct confrontation with and representation of natural detail. Many artists of both sexes went through this type of phase, and the pristine clarity of Francesca Alexander's floral decorations, Boyle's microscopic, nested nooks of nature, and Bolingbroke's precise illustrations all fall into this category of natural still lifes rendered for publication. In addition to the sanctity of nature, the sacredness of religion was another common subject, found in Waterford's biblical frescoes and in Esther Faithfull Fleet's dazzling illuminations for *Te Deum Laudamus.*

By far the most insistent message or imagery communicated by women artists in the majority of their paintings pertained to the identity and perception of middle- and upper-class life. This is true in the Claxtons' impressions of contemporary life and rituals at home, shopping, and elsewhere; in the Hayllars' distinctively detailed pictures of home, sweet home in Castle Priory's handsome rooms, occupants, and objects; in Alice Walker's painful image of romantic distress; in Osborn's melodrama pitting a madonna-like governess against a bulldog-faced matron; in Ward's matriarch presiding over dinner; and in Solomon's poignant governess and witty rendition of "a fashionable couple." Much the same could be said of royal artists' impressions of daily life. In drawings by Queen Victoria and her daughters Princess Helena and Princess Victoria, there is a kindred sense of candor in portraying the pleasures of private life—from children and pets, travels, and personal surroundings to flights of fancy about knights and soldiers transposed from literary realms.

Women were also attracted to images of childhood and innocence, a point borne out in this exhibition by the works of Edwards, Greenaway, Allingham, Osborn, Ward, Waterford, and Morris. In Osborn's *Where the Weary Are at Rest,* the cult of childhood is also linked to that of death, another favorite theme. Lady Waterford's *Babes in the Woods,* on the other hand, illustrates the death of purity and innocence with a "still life" of children murdered by their avaricious male relative. Ward and the Hayllars used family children in their images, and in Ward's *The Crown of the Feast,* it is the mother who shares center stage with the flaming entrée; perhaps the eight children pressed around the table reminded the artist of her own brood. Even Beatrix Potter's spritely rabbit family qualify as surrogate children in their anthropomorphized and infantile behavior and in their humanized garments, speech, and emotions.

Foreign and rural peasants were other cosmeticized images of class filtered through a middle-class vision. Lady Waterford's *Haymakers* are not really intended to be interpreted as downtrodden agricultural laborers toiling in a sea of golden grain. In an even lighter vein Anderson's *Guess Again* pivots around the supposed playfulness of winsome peasant girls. Girlish innocence also prevails in Alexander's images of Italian females, who range from the pseudo-saintly to the intimidated; the latter sense of endangerment is found in her illustration "The Madonna and the Rich Man," in which the presence of a man in contemporary garb comes perilously close to suggesting the pedophilia of Ruskin.

Portraits of real, literary, and mythological women also were popular subjects. In straight portraiture Violet Lindsay's depiction of *Ellen Terry* and Jessica Hayllar's of *The Hon. Ethel Lopes* convey a directness of feeling and execution. Particularly compelling is Joanna Boyce's 1861 *Portrait of a Mulatto Woman,* in actuality a sitter named Mrs. Eaton who posed as well for Rossetti and Albert Moore. A rare woman of color (as either subject or maker) in Victorian art, Mrs.

Eaton is shown as possessing both considerable dignity and beauty; while in other paintings for which she modelled she plays the role of servant or subservient figure, here she is shown on her own as a model/sitter, ennobled with the demeanor and dress of a Victorian lady. Among the innumerable heroines cast from literature or mythology are those pictured by Siddal, whose women are often lugubrious or melancholy victims, seemingly trapped in suffocating spaces and relationships, as in *The Woeful Victory* and other drawings. Evelyn DeMorgan also created her own pantheon of goddesses, ranging from Ariadne, Hero, and Flora to personifications of Luna and Night and Dawn, and this kind of ingenuity and variability of feminized subject was also evinced by Eleanor Fortescue Brickdale. In numerous books she depicted countless solitary females with Pre-Raphaelite looks (e.g., Tennysonian heroines Enid and Elaine) and in 1919 was commissioned to create fifteen images for *Eleanor Fortescue Brickdale's Golden Book of Famous Women.* This nod to fame included Maud, Guinevere, Titania, Joan of Arc, Fair Rosamund, and others, some of whom share allied themes of female abandonment, thwarted affections, melancholy, and supernatural power found in works by Siddal and DeMorgan.

On a less abstract note, much could also be written about the subject of nineteenth-century women workers, who appear in the background of some works (e.g., in Ward's *Crown of the Feast*) and as a central figure in others. The latter is the case for Osborn's *The Governess,* Solomon's work of the same title, and Blunden's *Song of the Shirt.* Each of these is worthy of lengthy analysis, for each projects multivalent layers about its subject, the social condition to which it alludes, the literary associations it encompasses, the pathos of expression and drama it deploys, and the artist's construction of femininity. While none is openly radical or feminist in content, covert messages (intentional or not) are conveyed about the plight of the poor teacher, a victim of circumstance and even female mistreatment, and the downtrodden needleworker, molded in Blunden's image into a particularly long-suffering Christian martyr inspired by Thomas Hood's poem.[69] In addition to these signal works the three artists created others that explored the possibility of female heroism and fortitude in various guises: e.g., Blunden's *The Emigrants, A Sister of Mercy,* and *A Returning Penitent;* Solomon's *The Claim for Shelter* and *A Young Teacher* (in which Boyce's sitter reappears as an exotic Hindoo ayah); and Osborn's *Nameless and Friendless, For the Last Time,* and *God's Acre.*

The exceptions to the foregoing, mostly predictable, categories of subject matter are to be found partly in the sometimes iconoclastic images of Adelaide and Florence Claxton, especially the latter. A surviving album with some of their work raises tantalizing questions about what might be written about other women artists if more of their work had been preserved. The Claxtons, like Allingham, Edwards, Boyle, and Greenaway, made a living mostly in the commercial realm and in their many illustrations and paintings continually treated the subject of women throughout their individual and collective oeuvre. Sometimes their treatment was comic, even keenly satiric; at other times it was deadly serious and trenchant about the lives of middle-class women in particular. As a concluding example their work encompasses many of the themes already discussed, especially those of middle-class existence, women workers, and the female artist.

The two sisters worked for some of the same magazines (*The Period* and *The Englishwoman's Domestic Magazine*) as well as collaborated on assorted projects—e.g., for *London Society* and for illustrations in *The Illustrated Times* of "The Hours A.M. and P.M. in London." One scene shows a nursery dinner at 1 P.M. with a governess attempting to restore order among her charges, while the 1 A.M. counterpart stages upper-class entertainment and glamour at a late suppertime gathering. The Claxtons also produced special

Fig. 6 Adelaide Claxton, "The Daily Governess,"
London Society, 1862

calendar illustrations in tandem; Adelaide's
February—Ladies Gallery at the House of Commons
shows the segregation of lady visitors to
Parliament, while Florence's all-female *Shopping*
vignette is in obvious contrast to the all-male
gathering of *Four Intellects* which she also
delineates (both with an eye for humorous
content). Each sister moreover treated some
identical themes, e.g., the female artist and/or
intellect, seen as a homely, bespectacled, severe,
and mannish type amid frothy feminine
stereotypes in Florence's *Conversaziones* and
equally sternly and traditionally in Adelaide's
Christmas Belles. At different times they also
painted or drew images of nuns, sempstresses,

and governesses. The latter was the main topic in
Florence's "England vs. Australia" illustrations
for *The Illustrated Times* of 1863, while Adelaide's
image of "The Daily Governess" (Fig. 6) was
featured in the 1862 *London Society* (which three
years later reproduced her overworked female
pianist in "Ten Shillings a Night"). Florence's
"Twenty-Four Hours by My Lady's Watch" for
The Illustrated London Times of 1867 was also quite
unusual, providing an unfolding pictorial time-
line and spoof of how middle-class ladies spent
their daily hours (mostly being tended by servants,
mothering, seeing art, riding in the park, dining,
and partying). Adelaide, on the other hand, forged
an unforgettable image entitled "The Good Time

That's Coming" for *The Period* in 1860, a vignette in which females are shown as forerunners of modern counterparts in the roles of college graduates, barristers, liberated smokers, capable athletes, tyrants with househusbands, and aggressors leading men on the dance floor. Her undated *Plain Sister* drawing is also riveting, if only because it captures the social disadvantages of physical plainness for a woman and the pain of sibling rivalry.

The Claxtons poked fun at both sexes, whether at work or at play, and on some levels Florence's illustrations for *The Adventures of a Woman in Search of Her Rights* (Fig. 5)of 1871 are troubling because of the flippant, pejorative way that women are portrayed. From "normalcy" through the abnormality of trying on different lifestyles and attitudes, the female protagonist "in search of her rights" is the constant butt of jokes, whether as befuddled artist, emancipated woman, or fledgling doctor. At the end of this dreamlike sequence, this "errant" female emigrates to America, where she finally gains "respectability" through marriage, albeit (in another humorous jab) as one of many wives in the polygamous family of the Mormon leader Brigham Young.

Despite this comic finale to her work, it was Florence who seems to have exhibited the most soul-searching, acerbic, and incisive paintings about the plight of contemporary womanhood. In 1858 she had on display at the Society of Female Artists a work entitled *Life of a Female Artist,* which *The Athenaeum* said was worthy as "Jane Eyre [*sic,* meaning Charlotte Brontë] would have made had she painted instead of written."[70] While partly amusing in tone, its focus on the concept of women making art was highly topical and revealing. *The English Woman's Journal* described it as "a fit commentary on the whole exhibition" with its pictorial litany of "…all the aspirations, difficulties, disappointments which lead in time to successes."[71] The setting is a studio or ladies' class with a disconsolate woman with her painting ironically of "the ascent to the Temple of Fame";

her climb is ended, however, for she gazes in despair "at an enormous R. [for 'rejected'] on its back."[72] This canvas was followed in the next few years with other paintings that continued an informal series of examinations of the Victorian woman's life: *Female Life, The Rights of Women,* and *Women's Work: A Medley* (all of 1861), *Scenes from the Life of a Governess* of 1863, and *Broken Off* of 1866.

Women's Work was arguably the most radical and may well have been her masterpiece. Provided with a long description by the artist, the work includes "the four ages of man", along with an "ancient wall of Custom and Prejudice."[73] Three governesses, female emigrants, a servant and middle-class lady, a woman surrounded by legal documents and male advisors, and various artists are among the many figures cast in this composition, one of the most extraordinary Victorian images to flaunt custom and scrutinize, in the art world and society in general, the position of women in England. Not surprisingly, Claxton brilliantly forges a central irony by evoking the "four ages of man" to tell a tale of women, whose lives are typically subjugated to and defined in terms of male needs and mandates. Significantly, few of the female captives successfully leave their peculiar prison-like pit, although one artist has scaled to the top and perches there to draw from nature. Overall, women's work and roles are shown as almost universally unsatisfying and thwarted in this curious composition, which couches its deviancy in the safety of satire, not unlike Florence's approach in her clever and better-known parody of Pre-Raphaelitism, *The Choice of Paris.* As a result of the unnerving candor and even subversive messages communicated by *Women's Work, The Spectator* warned that:

> this specimen…is noticed in the hope of deterring others from the path Miss Claxton is pursuing…. Sermonizing on social topics is not within the province of Art…. If an artist has a superabundant flow of misanthropy, let

him [sic] at least discover some more appropriate vehicle for its display than an oil painting.[74]

By concluding with the Claxtons, there is an opportunity not only to partly break with conventional subjects, but also to emphasize the primacy of the printed or graphic contribution besides that of the painted oil or watercolor. This is fitting, since women made their living as much from illustrations for books, journals, and other publications as from easel painting. Claxton's shift in tone and subject also signals the way to future dissatisfaction with the status quo, feelings made apparent especially in her unprecedented vision of "women's work."

There are also some generational differences that prevailed, as Lady Waterford commented to her younger relative, for numerous significant changes in the social fabric of English life transpired in the last twenty-five years of Victoria's reign. Whereas earlier generations of women were inadequately prepared to create art or to deal with fame, by the end of the century education and honors were at least theoretically more attainable. This was in part due to the widening of spheres in the 1880s and '90s, when the symbolic New Woman and others strode into the art class, society, and elsewhere with increased self-confidence and in greater numbers. Yet they were less anomalies than the natural culmination of earlier women's efforts and footholds; despite these gains, even after 1900 separate but unequal conditions lingered both in art schools and critical domains, and the possibility of equal pay remained remote as well. While concessions and opportunities emerged slowly during the later Victorian period too and were accessible mostly to middle- and upper-class women, women's lives were still basically centered around family and male needs, not their own, and the right to work and produce art was continually part of the undeclared strife and the unmarked battleground.

From the artists in this exhibition arises not a single collective perspective but many diverse ones offering often different angles of response to the challenges of gaining an art education, establishing a place in the art world, producing art, and perhaps achieving fame as well. As has been shown, a composite biographical portrait is impossible to recreate, although some similar strands can be discerned as recurrently interwoven. Mostly, youthful precocity triumphed over adversity, due in part to the omnipresent and invaluable element of family support—by father, mother, brother, or other mentoring force to nurture and sustain talent and hope particularly during the critical early phases of development. For this essay, and indeed, for the many women whose work is included in this exhibition, perhaps fame was not the final goal as either a holy quest or an ultimate validation of worth. At times their self-effacement and naiveté were palpably antithetical to such pursuit, and this and other factors may frustrate modern audiences. Yet far from appearing as oppressed victims (like some of the female workers they portrayed), the women artists included in this exhibition mostly emerge as purposefully directed, self-reliant, disciplined, persevering individuals. In spite of overriding cultural disadvantages, they summoned inner strength, resourcefulness, and fortitude to sketch, paint, and draw powerful pictures of women's cultural tradition, history, and heroism, in the process forging often indelible images that are part of a seemingly endless iconological as well as ideological "struggle for fame."

ᔷᔷᔷᔷᔷᔷᔷᔷᔷᔷᔷᔷᔷᔷᔷᔷᔷᔷᔷᔷᔷᔷᔷ

1. Charlotte Riddell, *A Struggle for Fame* (London: Richard Bentley & Son, 1883), II, 229–230.
2. Riddell, I, 235.
3. Riddell, III, 201.
4. Riddell, III, 64.
5. Riddell, III, 65.
6. Riddell, III, 64.
7. Riddell, III, 240.
8. Riddell, III, 45.
9. Riddell, III, 45.
10. Riddell, III, 252.
11. Riddell, II, 123.
12. I am personally and professionally indebted to the numerous scholars who have successfully tackled this vast subject, especially Pamela Gerrish Nunn, Jan Marsh, and Deborah Cherry, who have thus made my task of information-gathering a great deal easier. Their fact-finding, statistics, and interpretive insights were invaluable and are reflected throughout this essay. Among the many outstanding sources from the last decade that explore this subject and were especially helpful are Deborah Cherry, *Painting Women: Victorian Women Artists* (London and New York: Routledge, 1993); Pamela Gerrish Nunn, *Victorian Women Artists* (London: Women's Press, 1987); Deborah Cherry, *Painting Women: Victorian Women Artists* (Rochdale: Rochdale Art Museum, 1987); Pamela Gerrish Nunn, *Canvassing: Recollections by Six Victorian Women Artists* (London: Camden Press, 1986); and Jane Sellars, *Women's Works* (Walker Art Gallery, 1988). Besides consulting innumerable nineteenth- and twentieth-century biographies, memoirs, or monographs on individual artists, other works that were very useful in preparing this essay and producing the biographical notes in the checklist include Ellen Clayton, *English Female Artists*, 2 vols. (London: Tinsley Bros., 1876); Clara Erskine Clement, *Women in the Fine Arts* (Boston and New York: Houghton & Mifflin, 1904); Chris Petteys, *Dictionary of Women Artists: An International Dictionary of Women Artists Born Before 1900* (Boston: G. K.Hall, 1985); Margaret Kelly, *The Painter Was a Lady: Works of the Victorian and Edwardian Eras from The FORBES Magazine Collection*; and Penny Dunford, *A Biographical Dictionary of Women Artists in Europe and America Since 1850* (New York: Harvester Wheatsheaf, 1990).
13. Nunn, *Canvassing*, p. 2.
14. On the issue of cultural and scientific perceptions of male genius, see Christine Battersby, *Gender and Genius: Toward a Feminist Aesthetic* (London: The Women's Press, 1989) and also Flavia Alaya, "Victorian Science and the Genius of Woman," *Journal of the History of Ideas*, 8 (April–June 1977), 261–280. On representations of this subject in Victorian art, see Susan P. Casteras, "Excluding Women: The Cult of the Male Genius," in Linda Shires, ed., *Rewriting the Victorians: Theory, History, and Politics* (London: Routledge, 1992), pp. 116–146.
15. I am grateful to Nancy Marshall, a graduate student at Yale University, for sharing her thoughts with me on women's accomplishments, creativity, and perceptions of art, especially in her work for my course and her paper entitled "The Art of Seeing: Amateur Drawing Manuals and the Construction of Women Viewers in Nineteenth-Century Britain."
16. Peter Bicknell and Jane Munro, *Gilpin to Ruskin: Drawing Masters and Their Manuals 1800–1860* (Cambridge: Fitzwilliam Museum, 1988), p. 14.
17. "Society of British Artists," *The Lady's Magazine and Museum of Belles Lettres* (May 1834), 298.

18. Mrs. Sarah Stickney Ellis, excerpt from *The Daughters of England* as quoted in Susan Waller, ed., *Women Artists in the Modern Era: A Documentary History* (London and Metuchen, NJ: Scarecrow Press, 1991), pp. 72–73.

19. The best details and tables of statistics on women artists in the nineteenth-century, their yearly entries, exhibition histories, etc. are found in Charlotte Yeldham, *Women Artists in Nineteenth-Century France and England* (New York: Garland Publishing Inc., 1974), 2 vols., *passim* and also in Nunn, *Victorian Women Artists,* pp. 113–118.

20. Untitled article, *The English Woman's Journal,* 1 (May 1, 1858), 205.

21. Nunn, *Canvassing,* p. 7.

22. A thorough accounting of the history of the Society of Female Artists appears in Yeldham, I, 88–95, and other exhibition societies are discussed in 71–87.

23. "The Exhibition of the Society of Female Artists," *Art Journal,* 20 (1859), 83.

24. The issue of nude models is addressed in Yeldham, Cherry, and Nunn and is perhaps epitomized by the following Victorian critic's pronouncement on the subject: "Women shouldn't study the anatomy proposed of the human form (without which to excell is nearly impossible) unless they lose more in delicate feeling than they gain in ability." From "Society of Female Artists," *Art Pictorial and Industrial* (1873), 44.

25. As quoted in Yeldham, I, 22.

26. For more details on one-woman exhibitions in England, see Yeldham, I, 114.

27. George Dunlop Leslie, *The Inner Life of the Royal Academy* (New York: E. P. Dutton & Co., 1914), p. 48.

28. Leslie, p. 49. Here he also explains how unattractive, older women were deliberately eliminated from the program for the supposed benefit of the institution.

29. For examination of the gendered challenges facing women in the art profession and critical realms, see, e.g., Paula Gillett, *The Victorian Painter's World* (New Brunswick, NJ: Rutgers University Press, 1990), pp. 133–191.

30. "First Day of the Royal Academy Exhibition," *Sharpe's London Magazine of Entertainment and Instruction for General Reading,* 9 (1856), 80.

31. As quoted in *London Society,* 12 (July 1867), 11–12.

32. Walter Shaw Sparrow, "On Some Water-colour Pictures by Miss Eleanor Fortescue-Brickdale," *The Studio,* 23 (1901), 31.

33. Sparrow, 32–33.

34. Sparrow, 32.

35. Sparrow, 32.

36. Sparrow, 32.

37. Sparrow, 33–34.

38. Sparrow, 34.

39. Sparrow, 36.

40. "Exhibition of the Royal Academy," *Art Journal,* 23 (1861), 169.

41. "The Royal Academy Exhibition," *Art Journal,* 22 (1860), 168.

42. As quoted in Paul Usherwood and Jenny Spencer-Smith, *Lady Butler—Battle Artist 1846-1933* (Gloucester: Allan Sutton Publishing Ltd., 1987), pp. 35–36.

43. See Jan Marsh, *The Legend of Elizabeth Siddal* (London: Quartet Books, 1989) for additional details on this artist's life and complex relationship with Rossetti, Ruskin, and the Pre-Raphaelite circle.

44. July/August 1857 letter as quoted in Virginia Surtees, ed. *Sublime and Instructive. Letters from John Ruskin to Louisa, Marchioness of Waterford, Anna Blunden, and Ellen Heaton* (London: Michael Joseph, 1972), p. 15.

45. January 1857 letter as quoted in Surtees, p. 90.

46. Undated c. 1857 letter as quoted in Surtees, p. 90.

47. Excerpt from Ruskin's *Academy Notes* as quoted in E. T. Cook and Alexander Wedderburn, *The Works of John Ruskin* (London: George Allen, 1903), XIV, 308.

48. Margaret Howitt, ed., *Mary Howitt: An Autobiography* (London: Isbister, 1889), II, 117.

49. Jan Marsh and Pamela Gerrish Nunn, *Women Artists and the Pre-Raphaelite Movement* (London: Virago Press, 1989), p. 169.

50. Clayton, II, 429.

51. On the subject of male patrons of women artists, see especially Cherry, pp. 97–99 and 103.

52. On the culture of matronage, see Cherry, pp. 102–104.

53. On co-wage-earning and other arrangements, see the long chapter on "family businesses" in Cherry, pp. 19–44.

54. Jan Marsh, "The Woeful Muse," *The Antique Collector* (April 1990), 59.

55. Clayton, II, 76.

56. As quoted in Marsh and Nunn, p. 107.

57. Fuller details on Allingham's life can be found, e.g., in Ina Taylor, *Helen Allingham's England: An Idyllic View of Rural Life* (Exeter: Webb & Bower, 1990).

58. [Anna Mary Howitt], "Sisters in Art," *Illustrated Exhibitor and Magazine of Art*, 2 (1852), 364.

59. As quoted in Marsh and Nunn, p. 117.

60. The unusual nature of this marital partnership is explored in Sheila R. Herstein, *Mid-Victorian Feminist, Barbara Leigh Smith Bodichon* (New Haven and London: Yale University Press, 1985), pp. 95–124 on "Friendship, Marriage, and an American Journey."

61. Cherry, p. 36.

62. On Boyce's "intense love of independence," see Marsh and Nunn, p. 50 for further commentary.

63. As quoted in Marsh and Nunn, p. 51.

64. See especially Cherry on the dynamics of women artists marrying fellow artists, pp. 34–38.

65. Marsh and Nunn, p. 111.

66. For more information on the wide range of subjects Victorian women artists tended to depict, see Yeldham, pp. 167–168 and particularly Cherry's examination of the multiplicity of domestic and other themes, pp. 120–163.

67. Insightful analysis of the treatment and phenomenon of landscape in art and the themes of rural poverty and country life as painted by Victorian women is offered in Cherry, pp. 165–175.

68. On rural retreats, artistic practices, and the cult of country cottages in art, see Cherry, pp. 175–183.

69. On the theme of women workers, see Cherry, pp. 153–159 and Susan P. Casteras, "'The Necessity of a Name': Portrayals and Betrayals of Victorian Women Artists," in Antony H. Harrison and Beverly Taylor, eds., *Gender and Discourse in Victorian Literature and Art* (De Kalb, IL: Northern Illinois University Press, 1992), pp. 222–224 especially. On governesses and sempstresses by Solomon, Osborn, and Blunden, see also Susan P. Casteras, *Images of Victorian Womanhood in English Art* (London and Toronto: Associated University Presses, 1987), pp. 110–117.

70. "Society of Female Artists," *The Athenaeum* (1858), 439.

71. As quoted in Casteras, "'The Necessity of a Name,'" p. 225.

72. As quoted in Casteras, "'The Necessity of a Name,'" p. 225.

73. For a lengthy exegesis of other aspects of this provocative and iconoclastic painting, see Casteras, "'The Necessity of a Name,'" pp. 226–229.

74. Untitled article, *The Spectator* (March 30, 1861), 333.

"No finger posts—no guides":
Victorian Women Writers and the Paths to Fame

LINDA H. PETERSON

In Charlotte Riddell's autobiographical novel *A Struggle for Fame*, a young Irishwoman moves to London with hopes of becoming an author. Riddell's heroine Glenarva Westley has written fiction since the age of fifteen when, motivated by a desire to help her impoverished father, she experienced a Romantic epiphany and took up her pen to write. From her rural home in Ballyshane she has sent numerous manuscripts to publishers in Dublin, Edinburgh, and London—all returned with polite notes of rejection. Now, living in London, she intends to meet publishers in person, convince them of the worth of her novels, and earn her place as a professional author.[1]

Riddell's novel combines two common Victorian myths of the woman writer: one the story of an undiscovered genius, awaiting the chance for publication and fame; the other a more practical account of struggling with editors and publishers to get work read and into print. The first version of authorship derives, in large part, from the lives of the Brontë sisters, especially as constructed in Elizabeth Gaskell's *Life of Charlotte Brontë* (1857) and in subsequent mythologized biographies. The second derives from accounts like Harriet Martineau's *Autobiography* (1877) and from the *künstlerromane* of many aspiring authors like Riddell.

Stories of the Brontës recounted the lives of three talented sisters (and one brother) living in remote Yorkshire with little society other than their own and little entertainment other than the stories, poems, and plays they wrote with and for each other. Charlotte, Emily, and Anne Brontë might never have made it into print had not Charlotte discovered, one day in 1845, a secret notebook filled with Emily's poetry and convinced her sisters that they ought to publish jointly a volume of verse. Unfortunately, that volume, *Poems by Currer, Ellis, and Acton Bell* (1846), went virtually unnoticed and unsold (except for two copies). But the sisters determined that they would continue to write—this time novels. Of the three works they produced, two were accepted for publication by Thomas Cautley Newby—Emily's *Wuthering Heights* and Anne's *Agnes Grey*, published together in three-volume format in 1847. Newby rejected Charlotte's novel *The Professor*, but she received such an encouraging letter of rejection from another editor, George Smith of Smith, Elder, that she immediately wrote—and had accepted—her immensely popular *Jane Eyre*, which also appeared in 1847.[2]

If the story of the Brontës told of native genius finally recognized for its worth, the story of Harriet Martineau told of a patient, determined, practical struggle to achieve professional status. Martineau began her career with an anonymous submission to *The Monthly Repository*, a Unitarian periodical edited by W. J. Fox (who also helped Robert Browning get started). When Harriet's article, "Female Writers on Practical Divinity," was read by her brother and discovered as her own, he urged her to pursue a literary career: "Now, dear, leave it to other women to make shirts and darn stockings; and do you devote yourself to this."[3] As Martineau explains in her *Autobiography*, she pursued her career as "a professional son" might have done, continuing to review for *The Monthly Repository*, writing didactic tales for religious publishers, and eventually going to London with the scheme for her *Illustrations of Political Economy* (1832–34), the series that finally brought her fame and financial security. In London,

Fig. 7 Alfred Croquis,
"Harriet Martineau,"
Fraser's Magazine, 1833

however, as she found herself "trudging many miles through the clay of the streets, and the fog of the gloomiest December I ever saw,"[4] she almost despaired of finding a publisher to take her work, and her *Autobiography* tells of the demeaning terms she was forced to accept to get the *Illustrations* into print.

These two versions of becoming an author—genius discovered, diligence rewarded—do not, of course, account for the many paths that Victorian women writers followed in their struggle for fame. In some cases, families and friends assisted with initial publication; in others, women entered and won literary prize competitions; in most, they began modestly, writing anonymous reviews, producing children's books, contributing poems and stories to ladies' magazines, or doing the drudgery of copy-editing and proof-reading as they worked their way through the ranks.[5]

Most of the poets relied on their families and friends to help them into print. Felicia Hemans's juvenile *Poems* (1808), for example, was printed by subscription when Hemans was not yet fifteen. This practice required that supporters assist in advance with publication costs, in return for which they received copies of the volume and the honor of being listed as a subscriber. (As the century progressed, this practice declined and became associated primarily with amateur production.) Apparently, young Hemans had more than fame in mind when she assembled her juvenilia. It is said that her profits went to buy a military uniform for her brother.[6] It is also said that Hemans's mother instigated and executed the project, perhaps because she saw an opportunity to advance the professional careers of both a daughter and a son.

Other women poets, too, launched their careers with the support, financial and emotional, of their families. Christina Rossetti's grandfather Polidori printed her earliest known poem, written at age twelve, on his private press, and also her first volume, *Verses* (1847), when she was seventeen. Years later in 1861, her brother Dante Gabriel worked behind the scenes to get her poetry professionally acknowledged through publication in the *Cornhill Magazine*.[7] Elizabeth Barrett's juvenile poem, *The Battle of Marathon* (1820), was also privately printed, in this case by her father. The copy in this exhibition was presented to a family friend, Miss Ridley, and dedicated to her father, "To him, to whom 'I owe the most'"; in general, the family circle treated Elizabeth as its young prodigy, addressing her as "Our dear Sapho"[*sic*] and "The Dear Poetess."[8] In relying on family support, Victorian women were scarcely different from their male counterparts. The £30 needed to produce Robert Browning's first volume, *Pauline* (1833), was provided by his aunt, Mrs. Silverthorne.[9] Tennyson's early *Poems by Two Brothers* (1827) may also have been subsidized by a generous aunt.[10]

Not all aspiring women could turn to their families for financial support. In fact, as the example of Hemans suggests, many turned to writing to supplement the family income. This pattern was especially common for prose writers and editors, whose work demanded less of genius, more of diligence, earnestness, and usefulness. Charlotte Elizabeth Phelan (later Tonna) began modestly as a volunteer contributor to the Dublin Tract Society, later writing full-length works for remuneration and becoming the editor of the Evangelical *Christian Lady's Magazine*.[11] The sixteen-year-old Letitia Elizabeth Landon (known to her readers as L.E.L.) began by supplying verses to her neighbor, William Jerdan, editor of the *Literary Gazette*, and eventually worked her way into the editorship of two ladies' annuals, Heath's *Book of Beauty* and Fisher's *Drawing-Room Scrap*

Fig. 8 Alfred Croquis, "L. E. Landon," *Fraser's Magazine*, 1833

Book.[12] George Eliot began by translating Strauss's *Das Leben Jesu*; by writing anonymous articles for the *Coventry Herald*, owned by her friend Charles Bray; and by serving as unofficial editor of the *Westminster Review* from 1852–54, during which apprenticeship she revised submissions and wrote many of the articles.[13]

A less glamorous tactic—but often quite remunerative—was to begin with children's books. The English historian Agnes Strickland and her sister Elizabeth took to writing juvenile literature when their father died from gout. Agnes wrote for various ladies' annuals and co-edited Fisher's *Juvenile Scrapbook* before she and her sister began their popular series *The Lives of the Queens of England* (1840–48), which they dedicated to the young Queen Victoria.[14] Another collaborative team, Mary and Anna Sewell, started—and stayed with—children's literature, perhaps because they found the work so satisfying and successful. Mary Sewell's ballad, *Mother's Last Words* (1860), sold over a million copies and was quickly followed with *Our Father's Care* (1861), which did nearly as well. Her daughter Anna Sewell's *Black Beauty: The Autobiography of a Horse* (1877), became an instant best-seller, translated into many languages and still in print today.[15]

Some women tried more ingenious means to get themselves heard—often with dramatic success. In addition to submitting anonymously to periodicals, Martineau entered a prize competition sponsored by the Central Unitarian Association, for which essays had been solicited for the conversion "of Catholics, Jews, and Mohammedans." Martineau set to work collecting materials, outlining, and writing her three essays, each one copied by a different hand to make it impossible for the judges to recognize their common author. As it turned out, Martineau won all three competitions, proving to herself that "I might rationally believe that authorship was my legitimate career."[16] Mrs. Henry Wood (neé Ellen Price) must have felt a similar legitimation when she won the prize of the Scottish Temperance League for her story *Danesbury House* (on view in the exhibition in its original 1860 prize edition). The contest she had entered called for "the best Temperance Tale, illustrative of the injurious effects of Intoxicating Drinks, the advantages of Personal Abstinence, and the demoralising operations of the Liquor Traffic."[17] The next novel Wood published, *East Lynne* (1861), which illustrated the injurious effects of marital infidelity, quickly became a best-seller and a much-dramatized tale throughout the rest of the century. Such were the success stories that fueled the efforts of young, would-be authors.

Despite stories of writers like the Brontës (or perhaps because they were *only* stories), professional authorship remained *terra incognita* for much of the century. When young Victorian women set out to pursue careers as writers, they did not always find ready advice or obvious models to guide them. In Riddell's *Struggle for Fame* this point is made clear by the publisher whom Glenarva Westley manages to interview. When she asks him about paths to success, he gives only this answer:

> *If I could publish a key to the problem you want to solve it would sell so well, I should never need to bring out another book. The land you want to enter has no itinerary—no finger posts—no guides. It is a lone, mapless country, and if you take my advice you will keep out of it. The pleasures even of successful literature are few and the pains many.*[18]

Aspiring women authors did not even have the possibility of applying to the writerly equivalent of the Royal Academy that excluded women painters for so long.

One of the reasons that paths to literary success seemed so obscure was that Victorian women inherited myths of genius from their Romantic predecessors—and "genius" meant something innate, not something learned or developed. As Mary Jean Corbett and others have explained, the primary fiction about nineteenth-century authorship "was (and is) that the man of genius is wholly his own product, an individual whose native abilities alone enable him to succeed."[19] Genius needed no advice or assistance on the path to fame; it provided no formulae to follow.

Some women, particularly the poets, capitalized on this myth by presenting themselves as youthful geniuses or infant prodigies. On the spine of Letitia Elizabeth Landon's *Poetical Works,* for instance, there appears the bust of a Sapphic poetess; above, a wreath of laurel leaves circles the

OUIDA.

" O fie ! 'tis an unweeded garden."—*Hamlet*, Act I., Scene 2.

Fig. 9 Linley Sambourne, "Punch's Fancy
Portraits: Ouida," *Punch*, 1881

poetess's head; beneath, lies her lute.[20] Landon meant visually to echo myths of the Greek poetess Sappho, the greatest of all lyricists, as well as to imitate the gestures of Madame de Staël's Corinne, whose poetic achievements receive public honors in a ceremony where she is crowned with a laurel wreath.[21] So, too, did the designer of Elizabeth Barrett Browning's *Poems of the Intellect and Affections* (1865) intend to invoke such myths with a frontispiece that shows a young poetess surrounded by five muses.[22]

More often, however, Victorian women writers replaced the myth of genius with a myth of domesticity—and this, too, obscured the professional aspects of authorship. According to the domestic model, a woman's writing was an extension of her domestic labor, an authorized reinterpretation of her role as moral teacher, advisor, and guide. Charlotte Yonge's father

articulated this view (somewhat negatively) when he told her that "a lady published for three reasons only: love of praise, love of money, or the wish to do good."[23] Clearly, William Yonge considered the first two reasons unacceptable for his respectable, upper-middle-class daughter: writing for money would have compromised her gentility; writing for fame, her femininity. But Yonge allowed Charlotte to write and publish moral tales on the condition that she donate her profits to charity—which she did.

Charlotte Elizabeth Tonna expressed a more positive version of literary domesticity in her *Personal Recollections* (1842) when she described her literary "employment" in the same terms that she described her teaching of Sunday School or her founding of a London mission for the Irish poor. It was all, in her view, work for "the Master," a way that Christians "may bestir themselves for the good of others."[24] Such literary work could occur in—and proceed from—a woman's home.

Whether women writers invoked myths of genius or domesticity, such myths obscured the actual facts of professional life from their readers. In her *Personal Recollections,* for example, Tonna never discusses her profits (which she fought to keep from her estranged husband) or her controversial editorship of *The Christian Lady's Magazine* (which provoked controversy when she began to write about political affairs). Such details would have demystified the image she needed to project and compromised her status as a respectable middle-class woman who did not need to write for money. Unfortunately, such mystification made it more difficult for other women who wished to pursue a literary career.

No doubt, advice about becoming a writer was passed on informally from family members and friends, from "old boys" and "old girls" to aspiring young women. We get a sense of this informal network from Laetitia-Matilda Hawkins's comment about another female writer, Mary Robinson: she "became literary," Hawkins writes, and "brought up her daughter literary."[25] Similarly "literary," William Thackeray helped his daughter Annie (later Lady Ritchie) get started by publishing her work in the *Cornhill Magazine,* which he edited. Captain Frederick Marryat, the adventure novelist known for such books as *Frank Mildmay, or the Naval Officer* (1829) and *Mr. Midshipman Easy* (1836), must have been a superb advice-giver, for four of his daughters became novelists: Augusta, Blanche, Emilia, and Florence (the last of whose novel, *Fighting the Air,* is exhibited and gives a fictionalized portrait of herself and Augusta). Sometimes the advisor was a family friend. Rhoda Broughton, niece of the Irish novelist Sheridan LeFanu, encouraged the association of Mary Cholmondeley with her publisher, Richard Bentley. Bentley brought out Cholmondeley's early fiction in his magazine, *Temple Bar,* and later published her novels. (One suspects, however, that Cholmondeley never knew

Bentley was paying her £400 for the copyright of a novel while he was typically paying Broughton £1300–1500.)[26]

By the 1860s information about becoming an author became less private and mysterious, more factual and public with the availability of memoirs and letters written by professional women. This increased information resulted, in large part, from the decision of women writers to acknowledge—and insist on—their professional status. Harriet Martineau's *Autobiography,* written in 1855 but released only in 1877, discussed in detail such professional matters as her method of composition, her negotiations with publishers, and her use of literary profits (they were *not* donated to charity, but spent to support herself and her mother and to build a permanent home at Ambleside in the Lake District). In a similar vein, Frances Power Cobbe's *Life* (1895) provides a long list of the periodicals to which she contributed, complete with names of the editors with whom she worked. Cobbe describes her journalism in London during the 1860s and '70s, asserting that, by the regularity and quality of her articles, she "proved, I hope, once and for all, that a woman may be relied on as a journalist no less than a man."[27] In fact, Eliza Lynn Linton had proved the same point in the 1850s when she held a job reporting for the *Morning Chronicle*—but repeated proofs never hurt.[28]

Martineau and Cobbe (but not Linton) were part of a larger group of women writers, editors, and publishers who, beginning in the 1860s, worked actively to improve women's access to the professions. One group of activists, which included Jessie Boucherett, Adelaide Proctor, Bessie Parkes, and Emily Faithfull, helped to found the Society for the Promotion of the Employment of Women. One of its projects was the training of female compositors to work at the Victoria Press, opened in March 1860. The involvement of women not only in the writing but also in producing books set off a controversy in the newspapers, with male compositors leading the opposition and claiming (then as now) that working women took away men's livelihood. Despite controversy, the Press survived and won the approval of Queen Victoria, who designated Faithfull as "Printer and Publisher in Ordinary to Her Majesty."[29]

Increased advice and active encouragement of women's professionalism helped aspiring authors, but it was never easy for a Victorian woman to pursue a literary career *and* marriage. In a typical mode Dinah Mulock Craik's husband, business manager of and later partner in Macmillan, opposed his wife's writing novels after they were married.[30] In *A Struggle for Fame* the narrator comments: "There never yet lived a wise man who wished women to turn artists, or actresses, or authors."[31] Although the comment may be presumed to reflect the view of Mr. Lacere, Glenarva's future husband, it may also reveal Riddell's ambivalence about her own career as well. Nonetheless, many husbands actively supported their wives' work—including George Henry Lewes, who encouraged George Eliot to try her hand at fiction, and Robert Browning, who exultantly watched his wife's "divine book" *Aurora Leigh* go into edition after edition while his own *Men and Women* languished.[32]

If a woman writer might combine a literary career with marriage, even women themselves thought it undesirable to combine a career with motherhood. As Elaine Showalter notes, "Frances Power Cobbe, a high-powered feminist reformer who never married, insisted that mothers should not try to work outside the domestic sphere until their families were grown."[33] Elizabeth Gaskell advised a young mother and would-be author to wait until her children were older: "When you are forty, and if you have a gift of being an authoress you will write ten times as good a novel as you could do now, just because you will have gone through so much more of the interests of a wife and mother."[34] It was not until 1893 that women got matter-of-fact advice on combining marriage, motherhood, and career in Emily Crawford's

"Journalism as a Profession for Women." The advice was to get a good housekeeper and send the children to school.[35]

৯৯৯৯৯৯৯৯৯৯৯৯৯৯৯৯৯৯৯৯৯৯

Whether or not women writers received adequate advice and encouragement, once started many managed their careers quite well. Charlotte Riddell's heroine Glenarva may have succumbed to the allures of fame and lost herself in a social whirl that eventually harmed her reputation and literary production, but most women held a steady, professional course. Notable in this regard was Harriet Martineau, who not only made up schedules to keep herself on track but also produced detailed anecdotes, in a long chapter of her *Autobiography,* to prove that it was male authors who more readily fell prey to vanity and its consequences.[36]

A first step in managing a professional career was, for some women, the choice of a name. Although many simply used their family and married names, others invented male pseudonyms at the start. Charlotte Brontë explained that she and her sisters chose Currer, Acton, and Ellis Bell because "we had a vague impression that authoresses are liable to be looked on with prejudice; we had noticed how critics sometimes use for their chastisement the weapon of personality, and for their reward, a flattery, which is not true praise."[37] George Eliot's well-known disdain for "Silly Novels by Lady Novelists," as well as her desire for anonymity lest she fail in her first attempt at fiction, helps explain her use of a pseudonym.[38]

In the 1880s and '90s women seem to have turned to male pseudonyms in unprecedented numbers: Ralph Iron (Olive Schreiner), Lucas Malet (Mary Kingsley), Lanoe Falconer (Mary Elizabeth Hawker), G. Noel Hatton (Mona Caird), Vernon Lee (Violet Paget), George Egerton (Mary Chavelita Dunne), Maxwell Gray (Mary Gleed), Martin Ross (Violet Martin), Geilles Herring

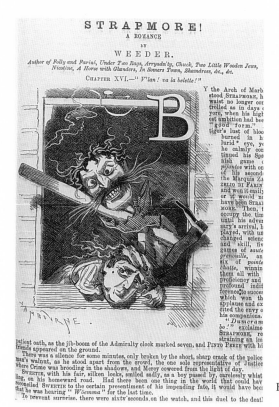

Fig. 10 Francis Burnard, "Strapmore! A Romance by Weeder," *Punch*, 1878

(Edith Somerville), John Oliver Hobbes (Pearl Craigie), Michael Field (Katherine Bradley and Edith Cooper), to name only some. Elaine Showalter has suggested that these pseudonyms allowed women "to represent everything in their personalities that transcended the cramping feminine ideal."[39] It may also be the case, given the turn against female novelists in the 1890s, that women adopted male names out of necessity. As Gaye Tuchman has recently shown, in the later nineteenth century good publishers like Macmillan came increasingly to reject women's manuscripts and publish men's, especially in the genre she calls "the high-culture novel." If a woman didn't want to be dismissed as a "lady novelist," she may have decided that the best protection was a manly name.

Beyond names, women writers often managed (or tried to) the visual images that were circulated of them and their work. The most famous instance of such visual management involved the Countess of Blessington, whose portrait became the frontispiece for Heath's *Book of Beauty* in 1834, the year she became its editor. Portraits of poetesses also supplied the frontispieces for collected works or retrospective volumes. In hers, Letitia Elizabeth Landon (L.E.L.) fostered the image of *une jeune fille* or of a modern Sapphic artist: one commonly-reproduced portrait shows Landon with round face, sweet eyes, rosy cheeks, and youthful dress (used even when she was in her mid-thirties); a more famous portrait (Fig. 8) shows her with hair *à la* Sappho, as Disraeli described it, and holding a rose, the flower sacred to the Greek poetess. Poets like Felicia Hemans and Elizabeth Barrett Browning chose more domestic, feminine images; indeed, it was common in collections of Hemans's poems to reproduce not only her portrait, but an engraving of the house in which she was born. With Christina Rossetti the visual image became art—but in this case, Dante Gabriel Rossetti's art, since it was his Pre-Raphaelite images of his sister that circulated publicly.

Prose writers had less to do with visual self-presentation. Most novels and essays were published without illustrations, let alone frontispiece portraits; the latter usually appeared only in posthumous biographies or collections. The famous image (Fig. 7) of Harriet Martineau in *Fraser's Magazine* (1833)—with feet on fender, cat on back, and pen in hand—was instigated by the magazine for its "Gallery of Literary Characters,"[40] the same series that featured Letitia Elizabeth Landon in 1833. (*Fraser's* had reviewed Martineau's *Illustrations of Political Economy* in less flattering terms than it had Landon's poetry, which may account for its less flattering portrait of a "professional" female writer.) The visual images of Ouida in *Punch* (Fig. 9) appeared without her consent or control, but indirectly, we might say, she contributed to their making. It was she who created the towering, aristocratic, and slightly ridiculous Strathmore, caricatured as "Strapmore" (Fig. 10), just as she, too, created her public image as an "aristocratic" writer, complete with mono-gram as coat-of-arms.[41] As the covers of her novels show, Ouida took much pleasure in promoting her self-created image and in working endless variations on the letters of her pseudonym.

What Victorian women writers had least control over was the thing most important to them: their books. In the worst cases, publishers brought out unauthorized or pirated editions for which the writers never received payment. This happened for instance, with an American edition of Elizabeth Gaskell's story, *Lizzie Leigh,* which was not only pirated but also attributed to Charles Dickens.[42] Some legitimate editions received not much better treatment. When Emily and Anne Brontë sold *Wuthering Heights* and *Agnes Grey* to Thomas Cautley Newby, they could not have expected a lavishly produced book: he had, after all, asked *them* to supply £50 toward production costs. They could, however, have expected to see an accurately printed text—something that Newby failed to deliver, even to the extent of ignoring the corrections in galleys that Emily had sent to him. With Smith, Elder, the publishers of *Jane Eyre,* Charlotte Brontë did better; although plain in appearance, at least the volumes were accurately printed. But, for the most part, women writers who published triple-deckers—the novels in three volumes so popular in the Victorian era and so essential to circulating libraries like Mudie's—could not expect to exercise much control over the physical appearance of their books.

In fact, the triple-decker format controlled women's writing much more than they controlled the results. Typically, a woman novelist sold her work and its copyright to a publisher like Newby, Tinsley or Bentley, who in turn brought out her novel in three-volume format. These triple-deckers were then sold to circulating libraries, which would loan the books to patrons one volume at a time. The system underwrote the profits of publishers (who sold the novels at high prices) and of the circulating libraries (who charged patrons a guinea or more for yearly memberships). The system tended to straight-jacket its writers: it dictated form and length; it limited profits; and since Mudie's, the largest circulating library, wanted material suitable for families, it limited even the content of books.[43]

The most successful of novelists, whether canonical figures like George Eliot or popular novelists like Ouida, did sometimes manage to control the material form in which their work appeared. Eliot's frustration at the limited space in Blackwood's for her novel *The Mill on the Floss* is well-known, but Eliot managed better with *Middlemarch.* She and her spouse, George Henry Lewes, decided that the novel should appear in eight separately-sold installments, a marketing technique Dickens and Thackeray had used with great success. They designed the wrapper of the separate volumes, a cover "crawling with vines and foliage and meaningless scrolls," as Eliot's biographer Gordon Haight has described it.[44] Haight thinks Eliot should have sought the counsel of her friend and painter Barbara Smith Bodichon, who had better aesthetic taste. After the release of the first issue, Bodichon wrote to Eliot:

I do not like the cover at all, it is not artistic enough—much better have nothing on the cover than that riggle and landscape, which are not worthy of your work at all. The green is not a bad colour, much better than the blue of the Spanish Gypsy, which was a very hard wicked blue and made me unhappy…. Do not let them do what they like in dressing your children[;] it does make a difference and I like to see your things in becoming clothes.[45]

Fig. 11   Aubrey Beardsley, title page for Florence Farr, *The Dancing Faun*, 1899

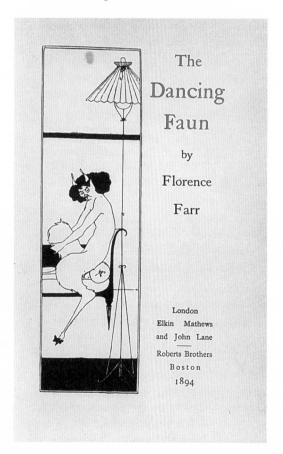

Viewers of the exhibition can make up their own minds about the design. Whether "artistic" or not, Eliot's wrapper signals that her work was meant to be high art, in obvious distinction to Ouida's which, with its lurid and sensational covers for novels like *Santa Barbara,* was meant to catch the eye of a different sort of audience.

As the century progressed, much more attention was paid to the appearance of novels —as one can see by following Rhoda Broughton's books decade by decade or by comparing the very plain first editions of Brontë's *Jane Eyre* or Gaskell's *Cranford* with the beautifully-produced editions of George Egerton's *Keynotes* or Ralph Iron's [Olive Schreiner's] *Story of an African Farm.* Egerton's collection of stories, with its cover design by Aubrey Beardsley, marks the impact of the Aesthetic movement on the publishing industry, as well as the specific tastes of her publisher John Lane. After the success of *Keynotes,* Lane instituted a "Keynote" series of books by women, including Florence Farr's *The Dancing Faun* (Fig. 11) (1899) and several other works by Egerton. Unfortunately, there may have been a disadvantage in being taken up by Lane who, known as "Petticoat Lane" because of his penchant for women, sometimes wanted more than publication from his authors.[46]

The most beautifully and lavishly produced books by Victorian women writers were, unfortunately but perhaps inevitably, published after their deaths. In the 1890s, for instance, Anne Thackeray Ritchie introduced a series of women's novels, illustrated by Hugh Thomson and published by Macmillan with gorgeous, gold-embossed covers; it included Mary Mitford's *Our Village,* Elizabeth Gaskell's *Cranford,* and George Eliot's *Scenes from Clerical Life,* to name only those in the exhibition. Implicitly, the series acknowledged that women's novels had become English "classics." Yet in its choice of titles it tended to emphasize the pastoral and domestic aspects of women's writing and to suggest that these aspects were the most important contributions that women had made to Victorian literature.

Even such a series as Macmillan's, however, does not match the lavish attention devoted to another Victorian classic: Elizabeth Barrett Browning's *Sonnets from the Portuguese*. As the privately-printed, hand-illuminated and illustrated editions in this exhibition suggest, the sonnets' story of love, romance, and married bliss captured the Victorian imagination and gave the poems an almost religious status. Some of these editions resemble missals or medieval bibles; in their lavish form they yet again suggest that women writers were likely to achieve fame—and retain it—by producing works that reproduced dominant cultural myths of romance and domesticity.

Most of the women writers in this exhibition did not achieve such fame, even after their deaths. Indeed, in Charlotte Riddell's *A Struggle for Fame* the relation of fame and death works differently. Glenarva Westley, the heroine, comes to associate her own literary successes with death—not her own but the deaths of loved ones, first her father, then her husband. At the end of the novel, as her husband dies, Glenarva thinks, "Once again FAME had crossed the threshold hand-in-hand with DEATH!"[47] Riddell's formula expresses the conflict that many Victorian women felt between their professional and domestic lives. Perhaps it also reminds us, in retrospect, of another formula that Riddell did not express: that death often destroyed whatever fame a Victorian woman writer might have had. It is an irony of this exhibition that the novel giving it its title has been virtually lost to history, only five copies known to exist in the United States, none on view here.[48]

1. *A Struggle for Fame* (London: Richard Bentley, 1883).
2. See Elizabeth Gaskell's *The Life of Charlotte Brontë* (1857; reprinted Harmondsworth: Penguin Books, 1975) and Winifred Gerin's *Charlotte Brontë: The Evolution of Genius* (Oxford: Oxford University Press, 1967).
3. Harriet Martineau, *Autobiography* (1877; reprinted London: Virago, 1983), I, 120.
4. Martineau, I, 165.
5. Among the accounts of Victorian women writers' struggles for professional acceptance, I have been most helped by these: Nigel Cross, "The Female Drudge," in *The Common Writer: Life in Nineteenth-Century Grub Street* (Cambridge: Cambridge University Press, 1985); Ellen Moers, *Literary Women: The Great Writers* (New York: Oxford University Press, 1976); Joanne Shattock, *The Oxford Guide to British Women Writers* (Oxford: Oxford University Press, 1993); and Elaine Showalter, *A Literature of Their Own: British Women Novelists from Brontë to Lessing* (Princeton: Princeton University Press, 1977).
6. Angela Leighton, *Victorian Women Poets: Writing Against the Heart* (London: Harvester Wheatsheaf, 1992), p. 9.
7. Mackenzie Bell, *Christina Rossetti: A Biographical and Critical Study* (Boston: Roberts Brothers, 1898), pp. 16–17; Georgina Battiscombe, *Christina Rossetti* (London: Constable, 1981), p. 98.
8. Leighton, p. 79. See also the copy of *The Battle of Marathon* (London: W. Lindsell, 1820) in the exhibition.
9. William Clyde DeVane, *A Browning Handbook,* 2nd ed. (Englewood Cliffs, NJ: Prentice-Hall, 1955), p. 10.
10. Robert Bernard Martin, *Tennyson: The Unquiet Heart* (Oxford: Clarendon Press, 1980), p. 45.

11. Charlotte Elizabeth [Tonna], *Personal Recollections* (New York: John S. Taylor, 1842), Letters V–VI.

12. D. E. Enfield, *L. E. L.: A Mystery of the Thirties* (London: Hogarth Press, 1928), pp. 51–54, 86–88. On the importance of ladies' annuals to the development of women's professional careers, see Alison Adburgham, "Writing Women of the 1830s," in *Women in Print: Writing Women and Women's Magazines from the Restoration to the Accession of Victoria* (London: George Allen and Unwin, 1972), pp. 249–272.

13. Gordon S. Haight, *George Eliot: A Biography* (New York: Penguin Books, 1968), Chapters II–III.

14. Shattock, s.v. Agnes Strickland.

15. See Marjorie Allthorpe-Guyton, "Artistic and Literary Life of Nineteenth-Century Norwich," in *Norwich in the Nineteenth Century* (Norwich: Gliddon Books, 1984), pp. 11–13

16. *Autobiography,* I, 150–56.

17. See the preface to Mrs. Wood's *Danesbury House* (Glasgow: Scottish Temperance League, 1860).

18. Riddell, I, 123.

19. *Representing Femininity: Middle-Class Subjectivity in Victorian and Edwardian Women's Autobiographies* (New York: Oxford University Press, 1988), p. 18. See also Marlon B. Ross, *The Contours of Masculine Desire: Romanticism and the Rise of Women's Poetry* (New York: Oxford University Press, 1989) and Christine Battersby, *Gender and Genius: Towards a Feminist Aesthetic* (London: The Women's Press, 1989).

20. *The Poetical Works of Letitia Elizabeth Landon* (Philadelphia: Jas. B. Smith, 1859). The portrait of Landon by Maclise also shows the poetess in a classical mode, with hair *à la* Sappho.

21. See especially Book II, "Corinne at the Capitol," in Madame de Staël's *Corinne* (New York: Albert Mason, 1875). Landon provided the metrical versions of the odes for the English translation of the novel.

22. *Poems of the Intellect and Affections* (Philadelphia: E. H. Butler, 1865).

23. Quoted in Showalter, p. 56.

24. Charlotte Elizabeth [Tonna], p. 241.

25. Laetitia-Matilda Hawkins, *Memoirs, Anecdotes, Facts, and Opinions* (London: Longman, Hurst, Rees, Orme, Brown, and Green, 1824), II, 33–34.

26. See the letters for 14 June 1888 and 2 September 1892 in the British Museum archives (46623, ff. 1–3, and 46624, f. 228), which give details of the contracts for Cholmondeley's *Sir Charles Danvers* and *Diana Tempest.* The contract for Broughton's *Alas!* guaranteed £1300.

27. *Life of Frances Power Cobbe by Herself* (Boston: Houghton Mifflin, 1895), II, 392.

28. Charles Dickens, commenting on Linton's work for his journal *Household Words,* said: "Good for anything and thoroughly reliable." Quoted by Vineta Colby in *The Singular Anomaly: Women Novelists of the Nineteenth Century* (New York: New York University Press, 1972), p. 16.

29. See Sheila R. Herstein, *A Mid-Victorian Feminist, Barbara Leigh Smith Bodichon* (New Haven: Yale University Press, 1985), pp. 140–141.

30. Gaye Tuchman, *Edging Women Out: Victorian Novelists, Publishers, and Social Change* (New Haven: Yale University Press, 1989), p. 43.

31. Riddell, II, 133.

32. William Irvine and Park Honan, *The Book, the Ring, and the Poet: A Biography of Robert Browning* (London: The Bodley Head, 1974), pp. 348–350.

33. Showalter, p. 67.

34. *The Letters of Mrs. Gaskell,* ed. Arthur Pollard and J. A. V. Chapple (Manchester: Manchester University Press, 1966), pp. 694–695.

35. Showalter, p. 68.

36. See the section "Literary Lionism" in Martineau's *Autobiography,* I, 271–374. "I had heard all my life of the vanity of women as a subject of pity to men: but when I went to London, lo! I saw vanity in high places which was never transcended by that of women in their lowlier rank" (I, 350).

37. Charlotte Brontë, "Biographical Notice of Ellis and Acton Bell," *Wuthering Heights* (1850; reprinted Harmondsworth: Penguin Books, 1965), p. 31.

38. Eliot's article "Silly Novels by Lady Novelists" was published in the *Westminster Review,* 66 (October 1856), 51–79.

39. Showalter, p. 58.

40. *Fraser's Magazine,* 8 (November 1833), 577.

41. For the caricatures of Strathmore, see *Punch,* 75 (1878), as well as their reproductions in Eileen Bigland's *Ouida: The Passionate Victorian* (New York: Duell, Sloan and Pearce, 1951).

42. See *Lizzie Leigh; and the Miner's Daughter.* Attributed to Charles Dickens (Philadelphia: T. B. Peterson, [1850], as well as Margaret Homans's discussion of the story in *Bearing the Word: Language and Female Experience in Nineteenth-Century Women's Writing* (Chicago: University of Chicago Press, 1986), pp. 226–233.

43. Gaye Tuchman describes the system in *Edging Women Out,* especially Chapters 2 and 7.

44. Gordon Haight, *George Eliot: A Biography* (New York: Penguin, 1968), p. 436.

45. Haight, pp. 436–437.

46. Showalter, p. 211, and Shattock, s.v. George Egerton.

47. Riddell, III, 346.

48. The *National Union Catalogue* lists five copies, three of them American editions in the Library of Congress.

ఖ-

The information for these entries has been
gathered from many sources, including
autobiographies, biographies, Victorian and
modern secondary sources, monographs,
exhibition catalogues, articles, and assorted
dictionaries. Whenever possible, birth and death
dates, as well as known or approximate dates of
publication or execution of works of art, are
indicated. Artists and authors are divided into
separate groups and arranged alphabetically
under the name by which they are currently
most commonly known. Unless otherwise noted,
individual objects belong to the collections of the
Yale Center for British Art; other collectors and
sources are cited.

CHECKLIST OF ARTISTS

Francesca Alexander (1837–1917)

Born in Florence, Italy, to an American portrait painter and his wife, Alexander attracted the attention of John Ruskin, who greatly admired her drawing style (comparing it to Leonardo da Vinci's) and encouraged her career. He edited her *Story of Ida* and brought out *Roadside Songs of Tuscany,* interpretations of Italian rural life which had been collected, translated, and illustrated by Alexander during her expatriate life in Italy.

Anunziatina Pasqui, 1856
Brown ink on cream paper (8 x 5 in.)
Lent by Mark Samuels Lasner

Rosina Bartolini, c. 1856
Blue-black ink on white wove paper (8 x 6 in.)
Lent by Mark Samuels Lasner

Illustrations for *Roadside Songs of Tuscany* (Pl. 1)
Translated and illustrated by Francesca Alexander
Edited by John Ruskin
London: George Allen, 1884

Helen Paterson Allingham (1848–1926)

Several women on the artist's maternal side were artists, including her aunt, who was the first woman to be admitted to the schools of the Royal Academy. Paterson studied and won prizes at the Birmingham School of Design, the Royal Female School of Art, and the Royal Academy. She successfully established a career for herself as an illustrator for such publications as *The Graphic, Once A Week, Cornhill Magazine,* and *Cassell's Magazine,* as well as for children's books before marrying the poet William Allingham in 1874. She exhibited primarily at the Old Watercolour Society as well as at the Fine Art Society and internationally in Chicago, Paris, and Belgium. She is best known for her beautifully rendered, pastoral, and typically nostalgic watercolors of rural England, and by 1903 over a thousand of her watercolors had been exhibited in London.

The Cottage Garden, c. 1878
Pencil and watercolor with Chinese white and scratching out (7 1/4 x 8 1/4 in.)
Lent by Mark Samuels Lasner

The Last House in Lynmouth, 1874
Watercolor with white bodycolor and gum arabic (7 3/8 x 10 11/32 in.)
B1986.4

Study of a Venetian Cobbler
Watercolor (5 1/2 x 6 5/8 in.)
B1975.4.811

Bluebells (Pl. 2)
Watercolor (11 1/2 x 9 1/2 in.)
Lent by Nicolette and Harold Wernick

Illustrations for Thomas Hardy
Far from the Madding Crowd
Serialized in *Cornhill Magazine,* 1879
Beinecke Rare Book and Manuscript Library

Sophie Gengembre Anderson (1823–c. 1898)

Raised in France until the late 1840s, Sophie Gengembre moved first to Cincinnati, Ohio, and then to Manchester, Pennsylvania, producing portraits and other paintings (e.g., for Louis Prang & Co.) before her marriage to the English artist Walter Anderson. The couple returned to Britain in 1854 and lived in London and Falmouth before moving to the Isle of Capri. Throughout her career she painted genre as well as portraits and some landscapes, exhibiting at the National Academy of Design in New York, at the Royal Academy from 1855–96, and at more avant-garde places such as the Grosvenor Gallery.

Guess Again, 1878
Oil on canvas (38 3/4 x 29 1/2 in.)
Lent by The FORBES Magazine Collection,
New York

Anna Blunden (1830–1915)

With a mother who was an amateur watercolorist, Blunden originally earned a living as a governess. She also trained at Leigh's Academy in London and began to exhibit in 1854 at the Royal Academy and the Society of British Artists, where this painting was on view. (It also traveled to America for an important 1857–58 exhibition of English art and may have been the work of the same title included in the Society of Female Artists in 1857.)

Inspired by John Ruskin's *Modern Painters*, Blunden began to correspond with him in 1855; Ruskin praised a few of her works in *Academy Notes* and gave her some commissions but personally discouraged her love letters and infatuation. After study and work in Italy from 1867–72, Blunden returned to England and married her deceased sister's husband, Francis Martino, subsequently exhibiting only at the Birmingham Society of Artists.

The Song of the Shirt, 1854 (Pl. 4)
Oil on canvas (18 1/2 x 15 1/2 in.)
B1993.23

Barbara Leigh Smith Bodichon (1827–1891)

A leading Victorian feminist from a wealthy liberal family, Bodichon was also a cousin of Florence Nightingale and knew many of the era's most prominent women. At twenty-one she achieved financial independence and supported a number of radical projects both before and after her marriage to a French doctor in 1857. (This sketchbook was created during their honeymoon trip to the United States.) A leader of the Married Women's Property Campaign in the same year, she helped start a ragged school and also co-founded with Emily Davies the eminent women's college, Girton, at Cambridge. In addition to her writing and political causes, she produced mostly landscape watercolors, having studied with William Hunt and attended drawing classes at the Ladies College in Bedford Square. She exhibited more than 250 works in London galleries from mid-century, especially at the Society of Women Artists, the Dudley Gallery, and the Royal Academy.

෪ම෪ම෪ම෪ම෪ම෪ම෪ම෪ම෪ම෪ම෪ම෪ම෪ම෪ම

Hastings Beach with Fishing Boats, c. 1850
Watercolor on paper (9 3/8 x 13 3/4 in.)
Lent by Mark Samuels Lasner

Elizabeth Siddal, May 8, 1854
Pencil on cream wove paper (4 15/16 x 3 3/4 in.)
Lent by Mark Samuels Lasner

Illustrations in *Louisiana Sketches,* 1857
Sketchbook
Beinecke Rare Book and Manuscript Library

Emily Bolingbroke (dates unknown)

Almost nothing is known about this artist, who collaborated with Mary and Elizabeth Kirby on this volume of semi-botanical text and illustrations of various specimens. Presumably Bolingbroke, like other women, was encouraged to draw natural history subjects because of her skill in delineating high degrees of detail.

෪ම෪ම෪ම෪ම෪ම෪ම෪ම෪ම෪ම෪ම෪ම෪ම෪ම෪ම

Illustrations for *Caterpillars, Butterflies, and Moths* by Mary and Elizabeth Kirby with illustrations by Emily Bolingbroke
London: Jarrold and Sons, 1860

Joanna Boyce (Wells) (1831–1861)

With a sibling (George Price Boyce) who encouraged her art and was himself a watercolor landscapist, Boyce became an ardent sketcher and was also influenced by Pre-Raphaelite art. She studied in London at Leigh's and Cary's and later in Paris with Thomas Couture; she also left a notebook attesting to her seriousness of purpose, her wide circle of acquaintances, and her desire for personal autonomy. One contemporary account noted that John Ruskin, who admired her painting *Elgiva,* had remarked on her "promising genius." Boyce somewhat reluctantly married a fellow artist, Henry Wells, in 1857 and continued to exhibit at the Royal Academy, the Society of British Artists, and elsewhere. Hailed by one reviewer in *The Spectator* as "the Elizabeth Barrett Browning of painting," she was at work on several paintings when she died unexpectedly and tragically after complications following the birth of her third child.

Portrait of a Mulatto Woman, 1861 (Pl. 5)
Oil on paper laid on linen (6 3/4 x 5 3/8 in.)
B1991.29

Eleanor Vere Gordon Boyle (E. V. B.) (1825–1916)

Largely self-tutored, Eleanor Gordon had lessons with a private drawing-master and others (including etching instruction from Thomas Landseer) before becoming a professional watercolorist and illustrator. Following her marriage to the Rev. Boyle in 1845, she illustrated many books and exhibited at the Glasgow Institute of Fine Art and the New Gallery. Her most popular book (which she also wrote) was *The Dream Book* of 1870.

Illustrations for *The Story Without an End* (Pl. 6)
by Sarah Austin
London: Sampson and Low, 1868

Illustrations for *Fairy Tales*
by Hans Christian Andersen
London: Sampson, Low, Marston, Low, and Searle, 1872

Eleanor Fortescue Brickdale (1871–1945)

An alumna of the Royal Academy schools as well as the Crystal Palace schools of art, Brickdale was one of the most successful illustrators of her day. Influenced by Pre-Raphaelite technique and imagery, she specialized in literary heroines, fantasy, and elaborate symbolic designs for a wide range of books, watercolors, and also some stained glass windows. By the age of thirty she had her own studio and later taught at Byam Shaw's art school. She exhibited at the Royal Academy and in Manchester, Glasgow, Liverpool, and elsewhere. Elected the first woman member of the Royal Institute of Painters in Oils as well as an Associate of the Royal Watercolour Society, she enjoyed solo shows and long articles dedicated to her work (e.g., in *The Studio* and *The Magazine of Art*) by the turn of the century.

A Cavern Scene
Watercolor (11 x 8 5/8 in.)
B1979.12.767

Rough Winds Do Shake the Darling Buds of May, 1900
Pencil and watercolor (15 1/2 x 10 3/8 in.)
Lent by Susan C. Ricci

In spring time, the only pretty ring time…, 1901 (Pl. 8)
Watercolor (15 1/2 x 10 3/8 in.)
Lent by Nicolette and Harold Wernick

The Introduction, c. 1909–11 (Pl. 7)
Watercolor (19 x 12 1/2 in.)
Lent by Susan C. Ricci

Illustrations for *Pippa Passes; & Men & Women*
by Robert Browning
London: Chatto & Windus, 1908
Sterling Memorial Library

Lady Butler, Elizabeth Thompson
(1846–1933)

The daughter of a gifted mother (both pianist and artist), Thompson also had a talented literary sibling, the poet and author Alice Meynell. In her youth Thompson took classes at the South Kensington School and at the Society of Lady Artists. In time, she not only won John Ruskin's highest, backhanded accolades because she allegedly painted like a man, but in 1879 she also unsuccessfully battled to become the first female elected to Royal Academy membership. Married to Major William Butler in 1877, she traveled extensively in Egypt and South Africa and later wrote of her experiences in her autobiography in 1923. Her large-format, detailed paintings of supposedly "masculine" military subjects gained her fame and audiences, including Queen Victoria as a patron.

On the Morning of Waterloo, 1914 (Pl. 3)
Oil on canvas (43 1/8 x 61 in.)
Lent by The FORBES Magazine Collection, New York

Cavalrymen Mounting Near a Fort
Watercolor (7 3/4 x 12 3/16 in.)
B1979.33

Mildred Anne Butler (1858–1941)

Born in Ireland as the daughter of an amateur painter, Butler in her early years studied with Paul Naftel, Phillip Calderon at the Westminster School of Art, and Norman Garstin in Newlyn. By 1899 she was exhibiting at the Royal Academy and continued to do so until 1902; some of her work was also shown in Ireland. In addition, her paintings were on view at the Royal Society of Painters in Water-Colours, the Society of Lady Artists, and the New Gallery. Mostly she produced watercolors and oil paintings, as well as animal, landscape, and genre subjects. Her watercolor entitled *Morning Bath* was bought by the Chantrey Bequest from the 1896 Royal Academy.

Nests at Kilmurry, 1886
Watercolor (21 x 14 in.)
Lent by Nicolette and Harold Wernick

Adelaide Claxton (1835/40–c. 1905)

Adelaide Claxton (who married George Turner in 1874), like her sister studied art primarily with their father, Marshall Claxton, and also briefly at Carey's School of Art. She became adept at watercolors as well as wood engraving and earned a living as a popular illustrator. Her interpretations of contemporary society appeared in such publications as *London Society, Brainy Odds and Ends, Bow Bells, The Period, Judy, Echoes,* and *The Illustrated Times;* for the latter she designed a noteworthy series entitled "Hours of the Day and Night in London." She also exhibited watercolors from 1863, although there is little trace of her works after 1876. She and her sister also collaborated on some commissions, e.g. "Illustrated Times: or the Hours A.M. and P.M. in London."

The Plain Sister (Pl. 9)
Graphite (4 3/4 x 4 7/8 in.)
B1993.31.21

Pouring Tea
Graphite (3 1/2 x 3 1/2 in.)
B1993.31.18

A Constitutional
Graphite (3 1/2 x 3 1/2 in.)
B1993.31.22

A Present
Graphite (2 7/8 x 3 5/8 in.)
B1993.31.19

Philippines
Pen and ink, grey wash and graphite (5 1/4 x 9 in.)
B1993.31.17

A Christmas Congregation (Pl. 11)
Graphite (4 3/4 x 7 1/2 in.)
B1993.31.23

"We Met"
Graphite (4 x 4 in.)
B1993.31.20

London Damsels
Wash and graphite (7 1/2 x 5 in.)
B1993.31.24

Christmas Belles (Pl. 14)
Wash and graphite (7 1/2 x 4 1/2 in.)
B1993.31.25

February—Ladies Gallery at the House of Commons (Pl. 12)
Engraving (6 1/2 x 9 1/4 in.)
B1993.31.38

Illustrations for *"Stage Whispers" and "Shouts Without"* by Charles H. Ross
London: Judy Office, 1881

Florence Claxton (fl. 1855–1879)

Florence Claxton, eldest daughter in the family, was also largely self-taught as well as tutored by her father. She and her sister accompanied him to Australia, Ceylon, and India in the early 1850s, and her sketches of some of these trips were later published. Like Adelaide (with whom she sometimes worked on illustration projects), she produced drawings and engravings for books, journals, and newspapers, including *The Churchman's Family Magazine, Good Words, The Illustrated Times, The Englishwoman's Domestic Magazine,* and *London Society.* She sent various works to the Royal Academy from 1859–79 and some of her watercolors were seen at the Dudley Gallery and elsewhere; a number of her most pointed paintings exploring the status of women were shown from 1858–66 at the Society of Female Artists. Although her output seems to have diminished somewhat after her marriage to Dr. Farrington in 1868, she still exhibited and drew, and the satiric *Adventures of a Woman in Search of Her Rights* of 1871 features a hundred witty illustrations by the artist.

The Third Volume (Pl. 10)
Engraving (3 3/4 x 4 in.)
B1993.31.44

Art Critics
Sepia wash and graphite (5 7/8 x 5 in.)
B1993.31.6

Conversazione
Graphite, wash, and bodycolor (4 3/4 x 8 in.)
B1993.31.11

Conversazione
Illustration for "A Conversazione at Willis's Rooms: 'The Artists' and Amateurs' Society'" for *London Society,* 1862
Engraving (6 1/2 x 9 3/4 in.)
B1993.31.12

Wallflowers
Pen and ink, graphite, and grey wash (5 1/2 x 7 1/2 in.)
B1993.31.16

Platts Spinning Machine
Engraving (6 x 9 in.)
B1993.31.42

The Choice of Paris, 1860 (Pl. 15)
Engraving (9 1/2 x 13 1/2 in.)
B1993.31.47

Shopping (Pl. 13)
Engraving (6 1/2 x 9 3/4 in.)
B1993.31.36

Four Intellects
Engraving (6 1/2 x 9 1/2 in.)
B1993.31.35

Crystal Palace
Engraving (6 1/4 x 9 3/4 in.)
B1993.31.37

Illustrations for *The Adventures of a Woman in Search of Her Rights*
London: The Graphotyping Co., c. 1871

Mary Darby (active 1850)

Little is known about Darby's life, although she seems to have been a pupil at one point of the versatile Edward Lear.

Godesberg on the Rhine, July 1, 1850 (Pl. 16)
Graphite touched with white on grey-green paper
(9 15/16 x 13 15/16 in.)
B1975.5.1805

Kilke, Ireland, January 20, 1848 (Pl. 17)
Graphite with white bodycolor (10 5/8 x 14 3/4 in.)
B1975.4.1804

Evelyn Pickering DeMorgan (1855–1919)

A talented prodigy hailed in her own time by G. F. Watts and others as "the first woman artist of the day," De Morgan studied originally with her uncle, John Roddam Spencer-Stanhope, and at the Slade School with Edward Poynter and was influenced by another artist in the Pre-Raphaelite circle, Edward Burne-Jones. From 1875–77 she studied and produced art in Rome. She married the ceramic artist and novelist, William DeMorgan, in 1887 and helped run as well as finance his pottery factory. A prolific artist and exhibitor at the Grosvenor Gallery and elsewhere (including at least one solo show during her lifetime), DeMorgan also finished two of her husband's novels after his death in 1917.

Nude Studies
Colored chalk on paper (16 x 23 in.)
Lent by The FORBES Magazine Collection,
New York

Study of a Woman's Head (Pl. 18)
Colored chalk on paper (12 1/2 x 8 1/2 in.)
Lent by Nicolette and Harold Wernick

Mary Ellen Edwards (M.E.E.) (1839–c. 1908)

Largely self-taught with only one term at the South Kensington School of Art, Edwards was part of a family of artists and throughout her career (and two marriages) exhibited at the Royal Academy (from 1862–1908), the Society of British Artists, and the Dudley Gallery. Besides painting floral and genre subjects, she was an accomplished draughtsperson whose illustrations appeared in *The Graphic, The Illustrated Times, Belgravia, Cornhill Magazine, Argosy,* and numerous books published by Cassell, Petter, and Galpin. For *Told in the Twilight* she collaborated on the illustrations with her second husband, John Staples, and most of her daughters also undertook artistic pursuits.

"Our Grandmothers" (Pl. 20)
from *The Graphic*, 1873
Hand-colored wood engraving (11 5/8 x 8 3/4 in.)
Lent anonymously

"One Touch of Nature"
from *The Graphic,* 1879
Chromoxylograph with aquatint (8 1/2 x 12 in.)
Lent anonymously

Illustrations for *Told in the Twilight*
by F. E. Weatherly
London: Hildesheimer and Faulkner, 1883

Esther Faithfull Fleet (fl. 1860s–1870s)

Fleet was the sister of Emily Faithfull, who published this book and many more at her Victoria Press, including *Thirty-Eight Texts Designed and Illuminated by Esther Faithfull Fleet* in 1872. This collaboration between sisters as artist and publisher/printer is one of many that occurred during the period.

Illustrations for *Te Deum Laudamus*
Illuminated by Esther Faithfull Fleet
London, 1868

Annie French (1872–1965)

French studied at the Glasgow School of Art and taught there from 1909–12; she also actively exhibited in Glasgow from 1904–24. A talented watercolorist, illustrator, and commercial designer of greeting and post cards, she married a fellow artist, George W. Rhead, in 1914.

The Bryde Heeds Not
Watercolor (8 1/2 x 8 3/4 in.)
Lent by Nicolette and Harold Wernick

Kate Greenaway (1846–1901)

Instructed in art by her father (a wood engraver), Greenaway received local art training under the national system at the Finsbury School of Art. She also studied at Heatherley's and the South Kensington and Slade art schools and won various prizes at the Royal College. She began exhibiting in 1868 and produced numerous commercial illustrations in the 1870s for *Little Folks* and *St. Nicholas* before achieving incredible success in the following decade. In 1878 she began working with the printer/publisher Edmund Evans, and the next year her book *Under the Window*, which she both wrote and illustrated, enjoyed instant fame and sold over 150,000 copies. Her illustrated almanacs, birthday books, and other children's publications were extremely popular and earned her international renown; her distinctive style was much imitated and reproduced on various merchandise from clothing to toys and china. Among her supporters were John Ruskin (who devoted an entire lecture to her at Oxford and corresponded with her for twenty years) as well as Queen Victoria, the Empress of Germany, and others. A member of the Royal Institute of Painters in Water-colours, Greenaway exhibited at the world's expositions in Chicago in 1893 and Paris in 1900.

Woman Fleeing with Child
Watercolor (11 1/2 x 10 1/8 in.)
Lent by Nicolette and Harold Wernick

Chromoxylographs for *Under the Window: Pictures and Rhymes for Children*
London: George Routledge, 1878–79
Beinecke Rare Book and Manuscript Library

Calendar pages for 1884
Beinecke Rare Book and Manuscript Library
Gift of Lansing V. Hammond

"Little Fanny"
Chromoxylograph for *Under the Window*, 1878–79
Lent anonmyously

"Five little sisters"
Chromoxylograph for *Under the Window*, 1878
Lent anonymously

Illustrations for *Mother Goose, or the Old Nursery Rhymes*, c. 1900
Lent anonymously

Elizabeth Gurney (c. 1820–1903)

Gurney was the niece of the eminent Quaker activist, Elizabeth Fry, whose prison reform efforts were chronicled in Gurney's diaries (and were later immortalized in paintings by Henrietta Ward and others). Later she married Baron Ernest de Bunsen and is the great-great-great-grandmother of Astrid von Heyl Forbes. Gurney's landscape views belong to a venerable tradition of outdoor sketching upheld by innumerable nineteenth-century artists of both sexes.

Devonshire Sketching Party
Pen and ink on paper (9 1/8 x 5 3/8 in.)
Lent by Mr. and Mrs. Christopher Forbes

From Duty Point, Devonshire
Pen and ink on paper (5 3/8 x 9 1/8 in.)
Lent by Mr. and Mrs. Christopher Forbes

Edith Hayllar (1860–1948)

Until her marriage to the Rev. Bruce MacKay about the turn of the century, Hayllar frequently contributed works to the Royal Academy from 1881–97, the Society of British Artsts, and other prominent institutions. She favored genre themes and often depicted the interior of her family's home, Castle Priory, Wallingford, from 1875–99. The Hayllar females were no doubt all inspired by the example of their father James, an artist who instructed his daughters in art. Some family members appear as figures in various works of art by Edith Hayllar and her sisters.

A Summer Shower, 1883
Oil on board (21 x 16 3/4 in.)
Lent by The FORBES Magazine Collection, New York

Jessica Hayllar (1858–1940)

An accomplished painter of genre scenes and mostly floral still lifes, Jessica Hayllar was confined to a wheelchair in about 1900 after an accident but still continued to paint until about 1915. She exhibited at the Royal Academy and other institutions, some in the provinces, during her career.

A Coming Event, 1886
Oil on canvas (22 1/2 x 18 1/2 in.)
Lent by The FORBES Magazine Collection, New York

Oriental Poppies and Coleus
Oil on canvas (10 3/4 x 7 1/4 in.)
Lent by Nicolette and Harold Wernick

Portrait of the Hon. Ethel Lopes, 1883 (Pl. 19)
Oil on paper (9 1/2 x 8 in.)
Lent by Nicolette and Harold Wernick

The Music Room
Oil on board (7 x 10 3/4 in.)
Lent by Robert P. Coale

Castle Priory—Interior, 1884 (Pl. 21)
Oil on panel (9 x 7 in.)
Lent by Susan C. Ricci

Kate Hayllar (fl. 1883–1900)

Focusing mainly on flower pieces and other still-life subjects, Kate Hayllar essentially seems to have stopped painting after she became a nurse in about 1900. Nonetheless, for several years prior to this her work was on view at the Royal Academy and the Royal Institute of Painters in Water-colours.

A Thing of Beauty Is a Joy Forever, 1890 (Pl. 22)
Watercolor (12 1/2 x 9 in.)
Lent by The FORBES Magazine Collection,
New York

Mary Hayllar (fl. 1880–1885)

A painter of landscapes and still lifes as well as genre and figurative subjects, Mary Hayllar mostly turned to painting miniatures after her marriage to Henry Wells in 1887. Her children served as models for some of her sisters' pictures, and she also painted subjects involving childhood.

For a Good Boy, 1880 (Pl. 23)
Oil on board (16 x 11 1/2 in.)
Lent by The FORBES Magazine Collection,
New York

Princess Helena (1846–1923)

The third daughter of Queen Victoria, Princess Helena was one of numerous women in the royal family who produced art. In 1866 she married Prince Christian of Schleswig-Holstein.

ఌఌఌఌఌఌఌఌఌఌఌఌఌఌఌఌఌఌఌఌఌ

Two Women Conversing
Watercolor (10 1/4 x 8 1/2 in.)
Lent by The FORBES Magazine Collection, New York

Anna Mary Howitt (1824–1884)

The daughter of authors William and Mary Botham Howitt, Anna Mary Howitt experienced bias firsthand as an aspiring artist before writing about such things in *An Art Student in Munich* in 1853 and *The School of Life* in 1855. Not long thereafter John Ruskin's negative assessment of one of her works evidently triggered a personal crisis for Howitt; and, although she continued to draw privately, Howitt ceased pursuing her professional ambitions as an artist and redirected her energies to spiritualism.

ఌఌఌఌఌఌఌఌఌఌఌఌఌఌఌఌఌఌఌఌఌ

Elizabeth Siddal, May 8, 1854
Pencil on cream wove paper (5 5/16 x 6 in.)
Lent by Mark Samuels Lasner

Jessica Landseer (1807–1880)

The daughter of an engraver and the sister of several artists (notably, Edwin, Charles, and Emma), Jessica Landseer painted numerous landscapes and miniatures as well as etched some works after her most famous sibling's paintings. From 1816–66 she exhibited various works at the Royal Academy, as well as sporadic contributions to the Society of British Artists and the British Institution. This rare juvenile work, inscribed on the back as by "Miss Landseer," was originally attributed to another (male) artist and at one point belonged to Jacob Bell, Edwin Landseer's friend and business manager.

ఌఌఌఌఌఌఌఌఌఌఌఌఌఌఌఌఌఌఌఌఌ

View of Colickey Green, Essex, 1817
Oil on canvas (14 x 17 1/2 in.)
B1986.11.2

Violet Lindsay, Duchess of Rutland
(1856–1937)

A talented watercolorist and sculptor, Lindsay produced many sketches and portraits (often in pencil or silverpoint) of eminent contemporaries such as Lord Curzon, the Countess of Oxford, Mr. Churchill, and Arthur Balfour. Her works were exhibited at the Grosvenor Gallery, the New Gallery, the Royal Academy, and the Paris Exposition in 1900. She was among the fortunate few to have a solo exhibition of her work during her lifetime, at the Fine Art Society, London, in 1919.

Ellen Terry in the Role of "Olivia," 1878
Pencil on cream paper (9 1/2 x 7 1/2 in.)
Lent by Mark Samuels Lasner

Lady Long, Amelia Hume Farnborough
(1762–1837)

Long studied notably with Thomas Girtin and Peter DeWint, producing mostly watercolors and drawings as well as etchings done during the Napoleonic War when she was with the troops that proceeded to Paris after the Battle of Waterloo. Her husband was Charles Long, who became Lord Farnborough in recognition of his work on behalf of the founding of the National Gallery in London. Lady Long was an active landscape painter, sending sketches and views probably like these examples on a regular basis to the Royal Academy from 1807–22. Three of her entries there earned her praise for her "superior talent in water-colour drawing" and revealed "a talent most uncommon in an amateur and worthy of a first-rate professor."

Old Church and House
Watercolor over pencil (14 1/4 x 10 1/4 in.)
B1977.14.5310

Jessie Macleod (fl. 1848–1874)

Macleod intermittently exhibited mostly genre subjects at the Royal Academy and elsewhere in the period 1848–74 and also occasionally collaborated with Mary Elizabeth, a pseudonym possibly for a relative or friend, on some publications featuring her illustrations and the poetry of her collaborator.

Illustrations for *Dreamland* by Jessie Macleod with illustrative lines by Mary Elizabeth
London: Kent & Co., 1859

Anna Lea Merritt (1844–1930)

This American-born artist received drawing lessons as a child and studied art while she lived in Paris, Rome, and Dresden. Later she wrote of the considerable influence on her career of her husband, art critic and painter Henry Merritt, who died in 1878, a year after their marriage. A prolific contributor for over thirty years at the Royal Academy, she also had works exhibited at the Royal Society of Portrait Painters, world's fairs, and even American institutions. Merritt was the first woman artist whose painting (*Love Locked Out*) was purchased by the Chantrey Bequest.

Ophelia, 1880
Oil on board (17 5/8 x 24 in.)
Lent by Robert P. Coale

May Morris (1862–1938)

The daughter of William and Jane Morris, both illustrious in Pre-Raphaelite circles, May Morris attended the South Kensington School of Design in 1880 and subsequently took a post at her father's firm as head of the embroidery department in 1885. She became involved in the formation of the Socialist League and wrote about embroidery and decorative arts following her marriage to Henry Halliday Sparling in 1890 as well as after their divorce. Towards the end of the century Morris emerged as a preeminent teacher and expert on embroidery and the decorative arts, exhibiting at the Arts & Crafts exhibitions between 1888 and 1931 and also establishing the Women's Guild of Arts in 1907.

Study from a Renaissance Drawing:
Head of a Girl, November 21, 1879
Pencil drawing (11 1/2 x 10 1/4 in.)
Lent by Mark Samuels Lasner

St. Cecilia, c. 1880
Pencil drawing (15 x 10 1/2 in.)
Lent by Mark Samuels Lasner

Emily Mary Osborn (1834–after 1913)

The eldest of nine children in a curate's family, Osborn was inspired and taught by her mother to become an artist and attended classes at Mr. Dickinson's Academy. Her first works were exhibited at the Royal Academy when she was only seventeen, and she continued to have paintings included there until 1884. Portraiture earned her money, but some of her genre subjects like *My Cottage Door*, *Nameless and Friendless*, and *The Governess* brought her fame and patronage. It was Queen Victoria who bought *My Cottage Door* and *The Governess*, and Osborn went on to win prizes and achieve success for her work—she even had two studios in London and Glasgow at one point in her career. In the 1860s she studied in Munich and produced numerous pictures with German themes. Later she exhibited at such prestigious places as the Grosvenor Gallery, the New Gallery, and Goupil Gallery.

Where the Weary Are at Rest, c. 1858 (Pl. 24)
Oil on canvas (12 x 10 in.)
Lent by Robert P. Coale

The Governess, 1860 (Pl. 25)
Oil on canvas (13 3/4 x 11 1/2 in.)
B1987.2

November Noon, Hoveton, 1885 (Pl. 26)
Oil on board (8 3/4 x 17 1/2 in.)
Lent by Robert P. Coale

Sailing Barges in an Estuary (Pl. 27)
Oil on board (10 x 18 in.)
Lent by Robert P. Coale

Beatrix Potter (1866–1943)

Another largely self-taught success story, Potter hailed from a family involved with art, and her mother was a watercolorist. Although she never exhibited and rarely sold a drawing, Potter became famous for her illustrations for the "Peter Rabbit" series and for her nineteen "little books" that were published between 1901 and 1913. When she married William Heelis in 1913, she had published seventeen books; later in life she retreated to the privacy of farm life. As with Kate Greenaway, her books continue to be popular even today and have spawned innumerable cards, books, stuffed toys, and other merchandise.

Study of Two Rabbits, c. 1893
Pen and ink and pencil on cream wove paper
(6 5/16 x 3 7/8 in.)
Lent by Mark Samuels Lasner

Two Rabbits Gathering Apples from a Tree with a Stick and Basket, c. 1893
Pen and ink and pencil on cream wove paper
(5 13/16 x 4 15/16 in.)
Lent by Mark Samuels Lasner

Anne Rushout (c. 1768–1849)

Little has thus far been discovered about this talented amateur artist, whose landscape views of various sites confirm her obvious ability to capture both topographical detail and the mood of landscapes. There are thirty-two watercolors and two pencil sketches in this volume, and the Center owns two other volumes by this artist which depict a wide range of English country houses, churches, monuments, and other places.

Views in a Collection of Drawings, Vol. 1, 1824–32
Watercolor over graphite (10 1/2 x 7 in.)
B1977.14.9506–9539

Emma Sandys (1834–1877)

The sister and daughter of artists (her brother Frederick was part of the Pre-Raphaelite circle), Emma Sandys often expressed a rather Rossettian aesthetic in her art, as conveyed by this portrait. Besides exhibiting various works at the Royal Academy between 1868 and 1874, she contributed to the Norwich Fine Arts Association and the Society of Lady Artists.

Portrait of a Woman, 1870 (Pl. 28)
Oil on panel (17 1/2 x 12 1/2 in.)
Lent by The FORBES Magazine Collection, New York

Elizabeth Siddal (1829–1862)

Until recently known primarily as a model for her husband Dante Gabriel Rossetti and other members of their Pre-Raphaelite group, Siddal was also a talented artist who worked initially with Rossetti and then enrolled in 1857 in the Sheffield Art School. Although Siddal was resistant to accept his assistance, John Ruskin showered her with praise and a stipend. Her plans to collaborate with Rossetti on a book of Scottish ballads never materialized, but her work was on view at the Russell Place exhibition in 1857 and on an important show of British art that traveled to America in 1857–58. Her numerous watercolors and drawings often treat lugubrious and medievalizing themes and are as melancholy in content as her poetry and her sad death from an overdose of laudanum.

The Woeful Victory, 1860
Pen and ink on cream paper (6 1/2 x 5 1/2 in.)
Lent by Mark Samuels Lasner

Study of Two Figures (Pl. 30)
Graphite (9 5/16 x 14 11/16 in.)
Bequest of Professor Richard L. Purdy
B1993.26.4

Rebecca Solomon (1832–1886)

The sister of fellow artists Abraham and Simeon (their mother was also an amateur artist), Rebecca Solomon studied with Abraham and also at the Spitalfields School of Design before embarking on a career as a professional painter. From 1850–69 her works were on view at the annual Royal Academy exhibitions and elsewhere (including the provinces), and she also sporadically produced copies of other artists' works (e.g., by John Everett Millais and William Powell Frith as well as by old masters) to earn a living. Although she had some critical successes with works like *The Governess* and *Behind the Curtain* (purchased by Baroness Angela Burdett Coutts), after about 1871 she seems to have suffered various health and other problems (in part due to the alleged "eccentricities" she shared with her brother Simeon) which contributed to her death.

Marie Spartali Stillman (1844–1927)

A pupil of Ford Madox Brown after 1864, Spartali Stillman also served as a model for others in the Pre-Raphaelite circle, notably Dante Gabriel Rossetti, Edward Burne-Jones, and photographer Julia Margaret Cameron. She exhibited at the Dudley Gallery starting in 1867, at the Royal Academy from 1870–77, at the Grosvenor Gallery, and in Manchester and Liverpool; her works were also seen in America at the National Academy of Design in 1875, the Philadelphia Centennial Exposition in 1876, and in Boston in 1904. In 1871 she married William James Stillman, an American journalist and editor of *The Crayon,* which championed Pre-Raphaelitism and Ruskinian tenets. The family lived in Italy and England, and the artist's daughter and step-daughter both became artists, at one point showing their works with their mother's at the New Gallery in London.

The Governess, 1854
Oil on canvas (26 x 34 in.)
Lent by Suzanne McCormick

A Fashionable Couple, 1854 (Pl. 31)
Oil on canvas with arched top (19 x 21 in.)
Lent by The FORBES Magazine Collection, New York

Orange Grove, possibly late 1870s (Pl. 29)
Gouache on paper (31 x 24 3/8 in.)
Lent by the Richard E. Brush Art Gallery and Permanent Collection
Gift of the family of Owen D. Young

Queen Victoria (1819–1901)

A patron of the arts (sometimes to women painters) as well as an amateur artist herself, Queen Victoria took drawing lessons from the noted animalier Edwin Landseer (and previously studied with Richard Westall and William Leighton) and also learned etching and lithographic techniques. More than fifty albums and sketchbooks filled with her drawings survive, dating from 1827 to 1890, and attest to her lifelong interest in art.

Study of a Veiled Woman with Hawk,
March 25, 1855 (Pl. 32)
Pen and brown ink over traces of pencil
on paper (9 x 5 in.)
Lent by The FORBES Magazine Collection,
New York

Princess Victoria, Empress of Germany (1840–1901)

The eldest child of Queen Victoria's large brood, Princess Adelaide Mary Louise was an amateur painter and sculptor who was active throughout her life and even had some works on display at the World's Columbian Exposition in Chicago in 1893. At eighteen she married Prince Frederick William of Prussia and established a studio in the palace where she painted numerous portraits of the imperial family. Some of her early sketches, like those by her mother, depicted family life at court as well as fanciful subjects.

An Italian Soldier Seated Outside a Tavern (Pl. 33)
Pencil and watercolor (10 3/4 x 14 3/4 in.)
Lent by The FORBES Magazine Collection,
New York

The Good Knight Bayard, 1856
Pen and brown ink, watercolor and bodycolor on
brown paper (13 x 9 3/4 in.)
Lent by The FORBES Magazine Collection,
New York

Princess Helena, 1863
Pencil heightened with red chalk on paper
(11 1/4 in. diam.)
Lent by The FORBES Magazine Collection,
New York

Still Life—Fruit in a Basket, 1873
Oil on canvas (16 x 21 1/2 in.)
Lent by The FORBES Magazine Collection,
New York

Alice Walker (fl. 1859–1862)

Few details survive about this artist, who evidently lived in London and exhibited one subject from the Arabian Nights at the Royal Academy in 1862. *Wounded Feelings* is known to have been shown at the British Institution the same year and explores a favorite Victorian theme of romantic betrayal and rivalry.

Wounded Feelings, 1861 (Pl. 34)
Oil on canvas (40 x 30 in.)
Lent by The FORBES Magazine Collection,
New York

Henrietta Mary Ada Ward (1832–1924)

The offspring of a family of several generations of artists on both sides (notably, her grandfather James Ward), Henrietta Ward was taught to draw by her mother, Mary Webb Ward (a miniaturist), and later studied at Sass's Academy and became adept at painting portraits, genre subjects, and historical compositions. In 1849 she married a fellow artist, Edward Matthew Ward, who was supportive of her career; their four daughters and a son all became artists too. In the early 1850s she was one of the first women to attend the Royal Academy lectures, and she exhibited at the Society of Female Artists from its inception in 1857. During this decade especially, her numerous Royal Academy entries earned her considerable praise and popularity. Although she exhibited at the R. A. for several decades (1849–1904), Ward lost her bid to become the first woman Royal Academician. Among her patrons was Queen Victoria, and female members of the royalty and aristocracy were among the students she instructed at her private studio at Lowndes Square and elsewhere.

"The Crown of The Feast" (Pl. 35)
from *The Illustrated London News*, 1868
Hand-colored wood engraving
(11 5/8 x 9 3/8 in.)
Lent anonymously

Lady Waterford, Louisa Stuart (1819–1891)

Born into an aristocratic family with a mother who was an artist, Lady Waterford also had a sister, Charlotte Canning, who was a watercolorist (and a lady-in-waiting to Queen Victoria). After she was widowed in 1859, Lady Waterford pursued her artistic interests and abilities, which were in time applauded by Edward Burne-Jones and George F. Watts; John Ruskin wrote her many letters (some discouraging), introduced her to the Pre-Raphaelites, and commissioned her to make some copies of old masters' works. Besides painting genre scenes, mythological, and literary subjects, Lady Waterford executed several frescoes in a village school in Northumberland. Later in her career her works were among those on view at the avant-garde Grosvenor Gallery in 1877–82, as well as at the Dudley Gallery and the Society of Women Artists.

The Haymakers
Graphite, watercolor, and bodycolor
(8 9/16 x 9 7/16 in.)
B1986.29.556

Illustrations and original watercolors
for *The Babes in the Wood*, 1849
London: publisher unknown, 1849

CHECKLIST OF AUTHORS

Isabella Beeton (1836–1865)

Journalist, domestic writer, and editor of the *Englishwoman's Domestic Magazine*, Beeton is best-known for her *Book of Household Management*, published serially beginning in 1859, in book form in 1861. Her book was so successful that she and her husband produced several sequels, including *The Englishwoman's Cooking-Book* (1862), a *Dictionary of Every-Day Cookery* (1865), and *How to Manage House-Servants and Children*, the last published after her death.

Mrs. Beeton's Dictionary of Every-Day Cookery
The "All About It" Books
London: Ward, Lock, & Tyler, 1868
Sterling Memorial Library

Marguerite, Countess of Blessington (1789–1849)

Novelist, memoirist, and editor of ladies' annuals, the Countess of Blessington achieved her literary reputation with the publication of *Conversations with Lord Byron* (1834) in the *New Monthly Magazine*. The Countess was a famous society hostess, her salons at Gore House also serving as the base for her editorial negotiations with authors for her annuals, *The Book of Beauty* (which she edited beginning in 1834) and *The Keepsake* (edited from 1841 to 1849). When her publisher went bankrupt, she was left with many of his debts and fled to the continent to escape her creditors, dying soon thereafter in 1849.

The Keepsake
London: Heath, 1849
Sterling Memorial Library

Mary Elizabeth Braddon (1837–1915)

Sensation novelist, journalist, and editor, Braddon is still known for *Lady Audley's Secret,* first published as a novel (1862), many times adapted for the stage. The novel and its successor, *Aurora Floyd* (1863), made her publisher William Tinsley rich and established her reputation as the most successful Victorian woman novelist in terms of sales. During the 1860s and '70s, in addition to producing virtually a novel a year, Braddon edited *Belgravia* and the *Belgravia Annual.* She was still producing novels at her death in 1915, though her later works were more psychological than sensational in mode.

Aurora Floyd
Lacy's Acting Edition of Plays, Vol. 58
London: Thomas Hailes Lacy, n.d.
Sterling Memorial Library

Belgravia, a London Magazine, Vol. 2 (1867)
Illustration by M. E. Edwards
Sterling Memorial Library

Anne Brontë (1820–1849)

Novelist and youngest sister of the novelists Charlotte and Emily Brontë. Her first novel, *Agnes Grey* (1847), was printed as the third volume of the original, triple-decker edition of *Wuthering Heights.* She also published *The Tenant of Wildfell Hall* (1848).

Agnes Grey
London: Thomas Cautley Newby, 1847
Beinecke Rare Book and Manuscript Library

Charlotte Brontë (1816–1855)

Novelist and sister of the novelists Anne and Emily Brontë, who wrote under the pseudonyms Currer, Acton, and Ellis Bell. Charlotte's first novel, *The Professor,* was rejected by several publishing houses, but an appreciative response from Smith, Elder encouraged her to write *Jane Eyre* (1847). That novel effected, in the words of her fellow-writer Margaret Oliphant, "a singular change" in English fiction. Brontë's other works include *Shirley* (1849) and *Villette* (1853).

Jane Eyre: An Autobiography
London: Smith, Elder, 1847
Beinecke Rare Book and Manuscript Library

Jane Eyre: An Autobiography
New York: Harper & Brothers, 1848
Beinecke Rare Book and Manuscript Library

Emily Brontë (1818–1848)

Novelist and poet, sister of Anne and Charlotte Brontë. Emily's only novel, *Wuthering Heights* (1847), appeared in print just before she died of consumption.

Wuthering Heights
London: Thomas Cautley Newby, 1847
Beinecke Rare Book and Manuscript Library

Rhoda Broughton (1840–1920)

Novelist and niece of the mystery writer Sheridan LeFanu, Broughton had a long, successful career writing triple-deckers for the circulating libraries. An early novel *Cometh Up as a Flower: An Autobiography* (1867), which like many of her works hinged on a plot of love versus duty, brought her critical fame and good profits, and thereafter she became one of Richard Bentley's best-paid authors. In the 1890s Broughton, unlike many other novelists, easily made the transition from triple-deckers to the new one-volume format, and she continued publishing (with Macmillan, who bought out Bentley in 1894) until her death. Her novels chart the material changes in the production of nineteenth-century books.

Nancy
London: Richard Bentley, 1873
Beinecke Rare Book and Manuscript Library

Belinda
London: Richard Bentley, 1883
Lent by Mark Samuels Lasner

Alas!
London: Richard Bentley, 1890
Beinecke Rare Book and Manuscript Library

Dear Faustina
London: Richard Bentley, 1897
Beinecke Rare Book and Manuscript Library

Elizabeth Barrett Browning (1806–1861)

Poet whose elopement with and marriage to Robert Browning have been immortalized in numerous editions of *Sonnets from the Portuguese.* An invalid for many years before her marriage, she gained popularity for such poems as *The Seraphim* (1838) and fame for such socially-conscious poems as "The Cry of the Children" (1843). After her marriage and move to Italy, she continued to address social and political issues in "The Runaway Slave at Pilgrim's Point" (1850), *Casa Guidi Windows* (1851), and *Poems Before Congress* (1860), as well as to complete her important narrative poem about the development of a woman artist, *Aurora Leigh* (1856). When the Poet Laureate William Wordsworth died in 1850, she was considered a possible successor.

The Battle of Marathon: A Poem
London: W. Lindsell, 1820
Beinecke Rare Book and Manuscript Library

Sonnets by E. B. B.
Reading: Not for publication, 1847
Forgery by T. J. Wise [London, c. 1893]
Beinecke Rare Book and Manuscript Library

Aurora Leigh
London: Chapman and Hall, 1859
Beinecke Rare Book and Manuscript Library

Poems of the Intellect and Affections
Philadelphia: E. H. Butler, 1865
Sterling Memorial Library

Sonnets from the Portuguese
Boston: Copeland and Day, 1896
Sterling Memorial Library

Sonnets from the Portuguese
Chicago: Ralph Fletcher Seymour, 1899
Sterling Memorial Library

Sonnets from the Portuguese
New Rochelle, NY: Elston Press, 1900
Sterling Memorial Library

Sonnets from the Portuguese
Portland, ME: Thomas B. Moser, 1901
Sterling Memorial Library

Sonnets from the Portuguese
London: George D. Sproul, 1901
Beinecke Rare Book and Manuscript Library

Mary Cholmondeley (1859–1925)

Daughter of the rector of Hodnet, Shropshire, Cholmondeley and her sisters grew up writing fiction. She published stories in the *Temple Bar,* edited by Richard Bentley. Bentley also published her first book, *The Danvers Jewels* (1887), a sensational detective novel. She is best known for the *künstlerroman Red Pottage* (1899), with its biting portrayal of the repression of middle-class women with artistic ambition.

Red Pottage
London: Edward Arnold, 1899
Lent by Mark Samuels Lasner

Frances Power Cobbe (1822–1904)

Writer on issues of social and religious significance, Cobbe began her career writing theological essays from her father's home in County Dublin. After his death, she traveled widely, worked in ragged schools, cooperated with other feminists to further women's causes and careers, and edited the anti-vivisectionist journal, *The Zoophilist.* Her *Essays on the Pursuits of Women* was dedicated to three professional women (an authoress, a sculptress, and a social reformer) and published by the all-female Victoria Press.

Essays on the Pursuits of Women
London: Emily Faithfull, 1863
Sterling Memorial Library

George Egerton [Mary Chavelita Dunne] (1859–1945)

Fiction writer and playwright, Dunne was perhaps the most influential voice among the New Woman fiction writers of the 1890s. Her collection *Keynotes* (1893), with its elegant frontispiece by Aubrey Beardsley, led to other collections with musical titles, including *Discords* (1894), *Symphonies* (1897), and *Fantasies* (1898). She took her pen name from one of her husbands, George Egerton Clairmonte, a minor writer.

Keynotes
London: Elkin Mathews and John Lane, 1893
Lent by Mark Samuels Lasner

George Eliot [Mary Ann Evans Cross] (1819–1880)

Essayist, translator, editor, and novelist, Eliot was the most impressive—and formidable—Victorian woman of letters. Eliot translated the influential German work of biblical criticism, Strauss's *Das Leben Jesu,* into the English *Life of Jesus, Critically Examined* (1846), and from 1852 to 1854 edited the *Westminster Review* with John Chapman. After her decision to live with George Henry Lewes, and with his encouragement, she turned to fiction, publishing her first book, *Scenes of Clerical Life,* in 1858. Her major novels include *Adam Bede* (1859), *The Mill on the Floss* (1860), *Romola* (1863), *Middlemarch* (1871–72), and *Daniel Deronda* (1876).

Middlemarch
London: Blackwoods, 1871–72
Beinecke Rare Book and Manuscript Library

Scenes of Clerical Life
London: Macmillan, 1906
Beinecke Rare Book and Manuscript Library

Sarah Stickney Ellis (1812–1872)

Fiction writer and essayist, Mrs. Ellis wrote the most widely-read conduct books for Victorian women: *The Women of England* (1839), followed by *The Wives of England, The Daughters of England,* and *The Mothers of England.* She was the daughter of a Quaker farmer and married the missionary William Ellis in 1837.

Family Secrets, or Hints to Those Who Would Make Home Happy
London: Fisher, Son, & Co., 1842
Sterling Memorial Library

The Home Life and Letters of Mrs. Ellis Compiled by her Nieces
London: J. Nisbet, 1893
Sterling Memorial Library

Emily Faithfull (1835–1895)

Publisher, editor, essayist, novelist, and women's rights activist, Faithfull is remembered today as the founder of the Victoria Press (1860), an enterprise that trained and employed women compositors, and the *Victoria Magazine* (1861), a journal devoted to publishing women's writing and pressing for greater employment opportunities for women. Queen Victoria honored Faithfull with the title "Printer and Publisher in Ordinary to Her Majesty."

Essays on the Pursuits of Women
By Frances Power Cobbe
London: Emily Faithfull, 1863
Sterling Memorial Library

Poems: An Offering to Lancashire
London: Emily Faithfull, 1863
Lent by Mark Samuels Lasner

A Welcome: Original Contributions
London: Emily Faithfull, 1863
Lent by Mark Samuels Lasner

Florence Farr (1860–1917)

New Woman novelist, later married to Edward Emory. With the success of Egerton's *Keynotes* (1893), the publisher John Lane began an entire series using that title, all by women and with twenty-two volumes designed by Aubrey Beardsley. Farr's *The Dancing Faun* was number 2 in the series.

The Dancing Faun
London: Elkin Mathews and John Lane, 1894
Lent by Mark Samuels Lasner

Michael Field [Katherine Bradley] (1846–1914) and [Edith Cooper] (1862–1913)

Poets and dramatists, Bradley and her niece Cooper began publishing poetry as Arran and Isla Leigh, the names on the early volume *Bellerophôn* (1881), included in this exhibition. With the publication of their first play, *Callirrhoe* (1884), they took the name Michael Field and under that name produced twenty-seven tragedies, most on classical and historical subjects, and eight volumes of verse. To their friends Bradley was known as "Michael," Cooper as "Field."

Bellerophôn
London: C. Kegan Paul, 1881
Lent by Mark Samuels Lasner

Elizabeth Cleghorn Gaskell (1810–1865)

Novelist and biographer of Charlotte Brontë, Gaskell began writing fiction after sixteen years of marriage and child-rearing. Her early novels, *Mary Barton* (1848) and *North and South* (1855), reflect her knowledge of life in industrial Manchester and her concern for the laboring classes. Other novels take up social issues that concern women, from the "fallen woman" of *Ruth* (1853) to the conflicts within middle-class families in *Wives and Daughters* (1864–66). Her best-known novel, *Cranford* (1853), depicts a community of women in a small rural English village.

Lizzie Leigh
Attributed to Charles Dickens
Philadelphia: T. B. Peterson, [1850]
Beinecke Rare Book and Manuscript Library

Cranford
London: Chapman and Hall, 1853
Beinecke Rare Book and Manuscript Library

The Life of Charlotte Brontë
London: Smith, Elder, 1857
Beinecke Rare Book and Manuscript Library

Cranford
London: Macmillan, 1891

Sarah Grand [Frances McFall] (1862–1943)

Novelist and suffragette, McFall adopted a feminine pseudonym to express feminist pride and self-confidence. Her two best-known novels are *The Heavenly Twins* (1893) and *The Beth Book* (1898), both feminist novels, the former advocating woman's right to independence, the latter drawing on McFall's own experience to explore the psychology of the woman artist. She became an active member of the Women Writers' Suffrage League and president of her branch of the National Union of Women's Suffrage Societies.

The Heavenly Twins
London: William Heinemann, 1893
Lent by Mark Samuels Lasner

Anna Mary Haweis (1852–1898)

Domestic and children's writer, Mrs. Haweis was the wife of a clergyman and author who published regularly with the firm of Chatto & Windus. She originally wrote and illustrated *Chaucer for Children* for her own son Lionel. She produced two books on home decoration, *Beautiful Houses* (1882) and *The Art of Decoration,* on view here.

Chaucer for Children
London: Chatto & Windus, 1877
Sterling Memorial Library

The Art of Decoration
London: Chatto & Windus, 1889
Sterling Memorial Library

Felicia Dorothea Browne Hemans (1793–1835)

Poet famous for her beauty and learning, as well as for her romantic and domestic lyrics, Hemans published her first poems in 1808 at the age of fourteen, in part to pay for the military uniform of a brother. In 1818 she began to write regularly to support her young family, after the somewhat mysterious desertion of her husband. Her most important volumes include *The Domestic Affections, and Other Poems* (1812), *The Forest Sanctuary* (1826), *Records of Woman* (1828), and the poem "Evening Prayer at a Girls' School," published in the *Forget Me Not* annual of 1826.

Poems
Liverpool: G. F. Harris, 1808
Beinecke Rare Book and Manuscript Library

Poetical Works. Ed. Mrs. L. H. Sigourney
Boston: Phillips, Sampson, 1853
Beinecke Rare Book and Manuscript Library

Geilles Herring [Edith Somerville] (1858–1949) and Martin Ross [Violet Martin] (1862–1915)

"Herring and Ross" were the early pseudonyms of the novelist-collaborators "Somerville and Ross." The two writers were second cousins who met while Somerville was working for *The Graphic.* On their first collaboration, *An Irish Cousin* (1889), "Ross" supplied most of the text and "Herring" the illustrations. The pair became famous for their comic stories of Anglo-Irish life.

An Irish Cousin
London: Richard Bentley, 1889
Beinecke Rare Book and Manuscript Library

John Oliver Hobbes [Pearl Mary Teresa Craigie] (1867–1906)

American-born novelist and dramatist, Craigie began to write and publish as a child, her first story appearing in a Congregational newspaper, *The Fountain,* when she was nine. During the first years of an unhappy marriage, Craigie turned to dramatic and art criticism for London periodicals. After separating from her husband, she published her first novel, *Some Emotions and a Moral* (1891), in Fisher Unwin's Pseudonym Library. For that occasion she invented the name John (for her father), Oliver (in memory of Cromwell), and Hobbes (for the English philosopher).

The Tales of John Oliver Hobbes
London: T. Fisher Unwin, 1894
Lent by Mark Samuels Lasner

The Dream and the Business
London: T. Fisher Unwin, 1906
Lent by Mark Samuels Lasner

Mary Howitt (1799–1888)

Editor, novelist, and children's writer, Howitt spent most of her professional life assisting her husband William. Together they founded and edited the short-lived *Howitt's Journal,* to which Harriet Martineau (among others) contributed. Together they wrote *The Literature and Romance of Northern Europe* (1852). Mary also edited *Fisher's Drawing-Room Scrap Book* and produced numerous children's books, including *The Children's Year* (1847) and *Our Cousins in Ohio* (1847). She was the mother of the novelist Margaret Howitt, who edited her *Autobiography* (1889), and the painter Anna Mary Howitt, who illustrated "The Child's Corner" in the volume of *Howitt's Journal* on view.

Howitt's Journal, Vol. 1 (1847)
Ed. William and Mary Howitt
Sterling Memorial Library

Geraldine Jewsbury (1812–1880)

Novelist, essayist, and writer of children's books, Jewsbury was extremely influential as the chief reviewer for *The Athenaeum* for three decades (1849–1880) and as a reader for the publisher Richard Bentley. Jewsbury's fictional career began with *Zoë* (1845), a novel unconventional in its religious and sexual views. On view is one of her children's books, according to the inscription "given as a prize for good conduct."

Angelo; or The Pine Forest in the Alps
London: Grant & Griffith, 1856
Sterling Memorial Library

Letitia Elizabeth Landon (1802–1838)

Poet and editor known by her initials, L.E.L. was famous for her love lyrics. Her most important long poem, *The Improvisatrice* (1824), is modelled, like her own life and career, on myths of the Greek poetess Sappho and on Madame de Staël's *Corinne.* Shortly after her marriage to George Maclean and her move to Cape Coast Castle, Africa, where he was governor, Landon died mysteriously of prussic acid poisoning.

Poetical Works
Philadelphia: Jas. B. Smith, 1859
Sterling Memorial Library

Vernon Lee [Violet Paget] (1856–1935)

Novelist and critic, Paget adopted a male pseudonym because she, like others, felt her work would only be taken seriously if she wrote as a man. She published her best-known book, *Studies of the Eighteenth Century in Italy* (1880), at the age of twenty-four. Her first novel, *Miss Brown* (1884), was a satire on aestheticism.

Studies of the Eighteenth Century
London: W. Satchell, 1880
Lent by Mark Samuels Lasner

Elizabeth Lynn Linton (1822–1898)

Novelist and journalist, Linton is best known for her series in the *Saturday Review, The Girl of the Period* (1867–68). Against her father's wishes, she moved to London to pursue a career as a novelist and, after a year reading in the British Museum, published the enormously learned *Azeth the Egyptian* (1846). When she discovered that she could not support herself solely by writing fiction, she turned to journalism, writing for the *Morning Chronicle* in the 1850s, then for the *Saturday Review*. She is reputed to be the first woman journalist paid a regular salary.

"The Girl of the Period"
Saturday Review, 1867–68
Reprinted London: Richard Bentley, 1883
Sterling Memorial Library

Florence Marryat (1838–1899)

Sensation novelist and youngest child of the popular adventure novelist, Captain Frederick Marryat, Florence was one of four sisters who wrote fiction. A prolific writer, she produced fifty-seven novels, most of them triple-deckers meant to be bought by circulating libraries. *Fighting the Air,* included in the exhibition, shows the labels of the famous Mudie's Select Circulating Library.

Fighting the Air
London: Tinsley Bros., 1875
Beinecke Rare Book and Manuscript Library

Harriet Martineau (1802–1876)

Didactic writer, novelist, and journalist, Martineau began her career as an anonymous reviewer for the Unitarian journal, *The Monthly Repository,* and as a writer of didactic tales for children. Her *Illustrations of Political Economy* (1832–34) brought her overnight fame and financial success. On a tour of the United States taken after the completion of that series, she wrote *Society in America* (1837) and *How to Observe Morals and Manners* (1838), now considered forerunners of modern social science. She was a vigorous proponent of women's rights, abolition, mesmerism, and Comtian philosophy and wrote regularly about these and other social issues.

Principle and Practice; or, The Orphan Family
Wellington: Houlston, 1827
Beinecke Rare Book and Manuscript Library

The Children Who Lived by the Jordan
Salem: Landmark Press, 1835
Beinecke Rare Book and Manuscript Library

Illustrations of Political Economy
Volume 4: Demerara
Volume 8: Cousin Marshall
Volume 12: French Wines and Politics
Volume 14: Berkeley the Banker
London: Charles Fox, 1832–34
Beinecke Rare Book and Manuscript Library

Alice Thompson Meynell (1847–1922)

A convert to Catholicism at the age of twenty-one, Meynell began as a poet, publishing her first volume *Preludes* in 1875. Her sister Elizabeth Thompson (Lady Butler) supplied the illustrations for that volume. Meynell turned to journalism after her marriage, in large part to assist her husband. She and Wilfred Meynell edited (and virtually wrote) the Catholic periodical, *The Weekly Register,* as well as the literary magazine *Merry England.* In the 1890s she wrote a weekly column for women in the *Pall Mall Gazette.*

Preludes
London: Henry S. King, 1875
Lent by Mark Samuels Lasner

Mary Russell Mitford (1787–1855)

Novelist, dramatist, poet, and children's writer, Mitford was also an important friend and confidante of Elizabeth Barrett Browning. Mitford's plays, *Foscari* and *Rienzi*, were popular in the 1820s. Her magazine sketches of country life were collected as *Our Village* (1832) and remain her best-known work.

᠀᠀᠀᠀᠀᠀᠀᠀᠀᠀᠀᠀᠀᠀᠀᠀᠀᠀᠀᠀᠀

Our Village
Introduction by Anne Thackeray Ritchie
London: Macmillan, 1893
Beinecke Rare Book and Manuscript Library

Margaret Oliphant (1828–1897)

Novelist, biographer, and journalist, Oliphant served as principal (if also anonymous) reviewer for *Blackwood's Magazine* for over fifty years. Her first novels depict life in Scotland where she grew up and draw heavily on oral tales passed down by her mother. Some of these novels, including *The Melvilles* (1854) exhibited here, were attributed to her brother, who in fact only served as copyist. Oliphant achieved great popularity, though not financial security, with her Carlingford series, which includes *Salem Chapel* (1863) and *Miss Marjoribanks* (1866). For most of her life Oliphant's earnings went to support her two sons and an extended household that included her brother and his children. *The Ways of Life* is the last novel she saw through the press.

᠀᠀᠀᠀᠀᠀᠀᠀᠀᠀᠀᠀᠀᠀᠀᠀᠀᠀᠀᠀᠀

The Melvilles
London: Richard Bentley, 1852
Beinecke Rare Book and Manuscript Library

The Ways of Life
London: Smith, Elder, 1897
Beinecke Rare Book and Manuscript Library

Ouida [Marie Louise de la Ramée] (1839–1908)

A self-named and self-created novelist, Ouida specialized in fiction of the aristocratic classes, particularly with a military hero or sportsman. Her most popular novels include *Held in Bondage* (1863), *Strathmore* (1865), and *Under Two Flags* (1867), all of which sold thousands of copies and were issued in cheap editions with sensational covers. *Punch* magazine parodied *Strathmore* as "Strapmore! a Romance by 'Weeder,'" no doubt increasing its sales. The original covers of Ouida's novels were often beautifully designed, with her monogram visible as a coat of arms.

Ariadne
London: Chapman & Hall, 1877
Beinecke Rare Book and Manuscript Library

Santa Barbara
London: Chatto & Windus, 1894
Sterling Memorial Library

Toxin
London: T. Fisher Unwin, 1895
Beinecke Rare Book and Manuscript Library

Charlotte Riddell (1832–1906)

Novelist and editor of *St. James Magazine* from 1867, Riddell chronicled the beginnings of her career in her autobiographical novel, *A Struggle for Fame* (1883). Like her fictional heroine, Riddell moved from rural Ireland to London, hoping to make her living by the pen. For the first decade she achieved only modest success, but with the publication of *George Geith of Fen Court* (1864) she was recognized as a leading popular novelist. Her novels, virtually all of them triple-deckers, include sensation and city fiction as well as ghost stories, the genre represented in this exhibition.

"Fairy Water: A Christmas Story"
Routledge's Christmas Annual, 1873
Beinecke Rare Book and Manuscript Library

Anne Thackeray Ritchie (1837–1919)

Eldest daughter of the novelist William Makepeace Thackeray, Annie (as she was called) began her career publishing essays in the *Cornhill Magazine*, edited by her father and later by her brother-in-law Leslie Stephen. She wrote novels steadily from her mid-twenties to the age of forty, when she married. Thereafter, she turned to biography and memoir and wrote prefaces to the series of famous novels by Victorian women exhibited here.

"Introduction"
Our Village by Mary Russell Mitford
London: Macmillan, 1893

Christina Rossetti (1830–1894)

Poet and religious essayist, Rossetti was the youngest child in a family of scholars, writers, and artists that included the Pre-Raphaelite painter Dante Gabriel Rossetti. Christina grew up writing verse, often in games called *bout rimés,* and was encouraged as a poet by her family, including her grandfather Polidori who printed her first volume, *Verses* (1847). Although she was not elected to the Pre-Raphaelite Brotherhood (on the grounds that she was a woman), she contributed to the PRB periodical, *The Germ.* She achieved fame with the publication of *Goblin Market* (1862) and at her death was considered the finest devotional poet of the century.

Goblin Market
London and Cambridge: Macmillan, 1862
Beinecke Rare Book and Manuscript Library

The Prince's Progress and Other Poems
London: Macmillan, 1866
Beinecke Rare Book and Manuscript Library

Olive Schreiner [Ralph Iron] (1855–1920)

᛫ᚦ᛫ᚦ᛫ᚦ᛫ᚦ᛫ᚦ᛫ᚦ᛫ᚦ᛫ᚦ᛫ᚦ᛫ᚦ᛫ᚦ᛫ᚦ᛫ᚦ᛫ᚦ᛫ᚦ᛫ᚦ᛫

Novelist born in Basutoland, Africa, Schreiner is best-known for her semi-autobiographical novel, *Story of an African Farm* (1883). During the 1880s when she lived in London, she also published *Dreams* (1891), a collection of allegories. She became a leader in the women's movement from the 1890s onward, her *Women and Labour* (1911) representing this aspect of her career.

Story of an African Farm
London: Chapman and Hall, 1883
Beinecke Rare Book and Manuscript Library

Dreams
Once a Week Library, April 15, 1891
Beinecke Rare Book and Manuscript Library

Mary Sewell (1797–1884) and Anna Sewell (1820–1878)

᛫ᚦ᛫ᚦ᛫ᚦ᛫ᚦ᛫ᚦ᛫ᚦ᛫ᚦ᛫ᚦ᛫ᚦ᛫ᚦ᛫ᚦ᛫ᚦ᛫ᚦ᛫ᚦ᛫ᚦ᛫ᚦ᛫

A mother-daughter team from the provincial town of Norwich, the Sewells gained regional and national fame as writers of children's books. After the birth of her first child, Mary wrote her first children's book, *Walks with Mamma*, in words of one syllable. Her collection *Pictures and Ballads of London Life* includes her "Mother's Last Words" (1860), which sold over one million copies, a sale unprecedented in the history of ballads, and "Our Father's Care" (1861), which sold almost as well with 776,000 impressions. Anna Sewell's still-famous *Black Beauty* (1877) was dedicated to her mother and has been in print continuously since its publication.

Pictures and Ballads of London Life
London: Jarrold and Sons, c. 1870

Black Beauty: The Autobiography of a Horse
London: Jarrold and Sons, 1877
Beinecke Rare Book and Manuscript Library

Agnes Strickland (1796–1874)

Novelist, children's writer, and historian, Strickland is known chiefly for her twelve-volume *Lives of the Queens of England* (1840–48), written in collaboration with her sister Elizabeth (1794–1875). In their early years Agnes and Elizabeth collaborated on children's books and together planned the *Lives* series. Why only Agnes's name appears on the title page, despite extensive contributions by Elizabeth, remains a mystery.

Lives of the Queens of England, Vol. 12
London: Henry Colburn, 1848
Lent by Nancy Marshall Strebeigh

Charlotte Elizabeth Browne Phelan Tonna (1790–1846)

Writer of religious pamphlets and didactic tales, Tonna began her career writing pamphlets for the Dublin Tract Society and moral tales for children and servants. Under the pen name "Charlotte Elizabeth," which she adopted to prevent her husband from confiscating her profits, she continued her career as a religious poet, Evangelical reformer, and editor of *The Christian Lady's Magazine*. Her tale *Helen Fleetwood* (1839–40) is an early example of industrial fiction.

Osric, A Missionary Tale
London: James Nisbet, 1826
Beinecke Rare Book and Manuscript Library

The Rockite, An Irish Story
London: James Nisbet, 1829
Beinecke Rare Book and Manuscript Library

The Christian Lady's Magazine
London: R. B. Seeley and W. Burnside, 1842
Sterling Memorial Library

Laura Jewry Valentine (1814–1899)

Children's writer about whom little is known, Valentine produced a number of books under the pen name "Aunt Louisa," including *Aunt Louisa's Sunday Picture Book, Domestic Animals, Four-footed Friends and Favourites,* and *The Good Little Scholar, or Mother's Birthday.*

Aunt Louisa's Nursery Favourites
London: Frederick Warne, 1899

John Strange Winter [Henrietta Vaughan Stannard] (1856–1911)

Journalist and novelist, Henrietta Vaughan began as a regular contributor of fiction to the *Family Herald*. She published her novels, most of them about military life, under the pseudonym John Strange Winter. Her best-known book, *Bootle's Baby: A Story of the Scarlet Lancers* (1885), appeared the year after her marriage to Arthur Stannard, a civil engineer to whom she was devoted. *Bootle's Baby,* first serialized in *The Graphic,* is said to have sold over two million copies in the first decade after its publication.

Confessions of a Publisher
London: F. Y. White, 1888
Lent by Mark Samuels Lasner

Mrs. Henry Wood (1814–1887)

Novelist who launched her career at the age of forty-six with *Danesbury House* (1860), a prize-winning submission for a competition sponsored by the Scottish Temperance League for the "best Temperance Tale, illustrative of the injurious effects of Intoxicating Drinks, the advantages of Personal Abstinence, and the demoralising operations of the Liquor Traffic." Wood is best-known for *East Lynne* (1861), a melodramatic tale of a fallen, then repentant wife which was frequently adapted for the stage.

Danesbury House
Glasgow: Scottish Temperance League, 1860
Beinecke Rare Book and Manuscript Library

Charlotte Yonge (1823–1901)

Didactic and historical novelist, Yonge was the
daughter of a wealthy clergyman and a disciple of
John Keble. She aimed to make her fiction embody
her High Church Anglican principles and did so
with enormous success—her well-known *The Heir
of Redclyffe* (1853) and *The Daisy Chain* (1856)
going into multiple editions and her collected
works being brought out by Macmillan in 1882.
Yonge never collected the profits from her novels.
At her father's insistence she gave the money to
domestic charities and foreign missions.

෬෬෬෬෬෬෬෬෬෬෬෬෬෬෬෬෬෬෬෬෬෬෬

The Heir of Redclyffe
London: John N. Parker and Son, 1853
Beinecke Rare Book and Manuscript Library

Heartsease
London: Macmillan, 1882
Sterling Memorial Library

ADVICE AND INSTRUCTION BOOKS BY AND FOR WOMEN
෬෬෬෬෬෬෬෬෬෬෬෬෬෬෬෬෬෬෬෬෬෬෬෬෬෬෬෬෬෬෬෬෬෬෬෬

Hannah Bolton
Drawing Objects
London: Groombridge & Sons, 1850

Emma Cooper
Plain Words on the Art and Practice of Illuminating
London: Gladwell, Richardson, & Co., 1868

B. F. Gandee
*The Artist, or Young Ladies Instructor in
Ornamental Painting, Drawing, etc.*
London: Chapman and Hall, 1835

Rosamund Marriott-Watson
The Art of the House
London: George Bell, 1897
Lent by Mark Samuels Lasner

Elizabeth Steele Perkins
Elements of Drawing and Flower Painting
London: T. Hurst, 1835

Mary Roberts
*Voices from the Woodlands, Descriptive of Forest
Trees, Ferns, Mosses, and Lichens*
London: Reeve, Benham, and Reeve, 1850

1 Francesca Alexander
Illustration from *Roadside Songs of Tuscany*

2 Helen Allingham
Bluebells

3 Lady Butler
On the Morning of Waterloo

4 Anna Blunden
The Song of the Shirt

5 Joanna Boyce Wells
Portrait of a Mulatto Woman

6 Eleanor Vere Boyle
Illustration from *The Story Without an End*

8 Eleanor Fortescue Brickdale
In spring time…

7 Eleanor Fortescue Brickdale
The Introduction

9 Adelaide Claxton
The Plain Sister

10 Florence Claxton
The Third Volume

11 Adelaide Claxton
A *Christmas Congregation*

12 Adelaide Claxton
February—Ladies Gallery at the House of Commons

13 Florence Claxton
Shopping

14 Adelaide Claxton
    Christmas Belles

15 Florence Claxton
    The Choice of Paris

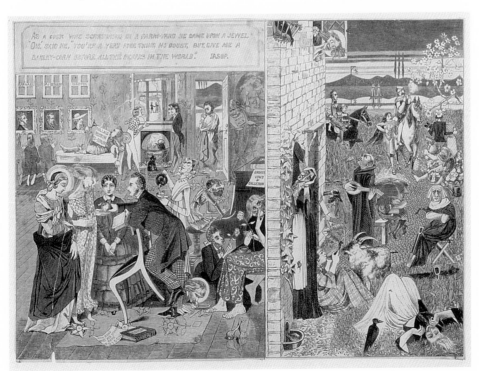

16 Mary Darby
    Godesberg on the Rhine

17 Mary Darby
    Kilke, Ireland

18 Evelyn Pickering DeMorgan
Study of a Woman's Head

19 Jessica Hayllar
Portrait of the Hon. Ethel Lopes

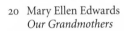

20 Mary Ellen Edwards
Our Grandmothers

21 Jessica Hayllar
    Castle Priory—Interior

22 Kate Hayllar
    A Thing of Beauty Is a Joy Forever

23 Mary Hayllar
    For a Good Boy

24 Emily Osborn
Where the Weary Are at Rest

25 Emily Osborn
The Governess

26   Emily Osborn
     November Noon, Hoveton

27   Emily Osborn
     Sailing Barges in an Estuary

28 Emma Sandys
Portrait of a Woman

29 Marie Spartali Stillman
Orange Grove

30   Elizabeth Siddal
     Study of Two Figures

31   Rebecca Solomon
     A Fashionable Couple

32 Queen Victoria
Study of a Veiled Woman with Hawk

33 Princess Victoria
An Italian Soldier Seated Outside a Tavern

34 Alice Walker
Wounded Feelings

35 Henrietta Ward
The Crown of the Feast